FOR ORGANS, PIANOS & ELECTRONIC KEYBOARDS

50

THE BEST OF
PATSY CLINE

CONTENTS

HAL•LEONARD®
CORPORATION

7777 W. BLUEMOUND RD. P.O. BOX 13819 MILWAUKEE, WI 53213

E-Z Play ® TODAY Music Notation © 1975 HAL LEONARD PUBLISHING CORPORATION
Copyright © 1991 HAL LEONARD PUBLISHING CORPORATION
International Copyright Secured   All Rights Reserved

E-Z PLAY and EASY ELECTRONIC KEYBOARD MUSIC are registered trademarks of HAL LEONARD PUBLISHING CORPORATION.

ISBN 978-0-7935-0509-8

Blue Moon Of Kentucky

Registration: 1
Rhythm: Swing

Words and Music by
Bill Monroe

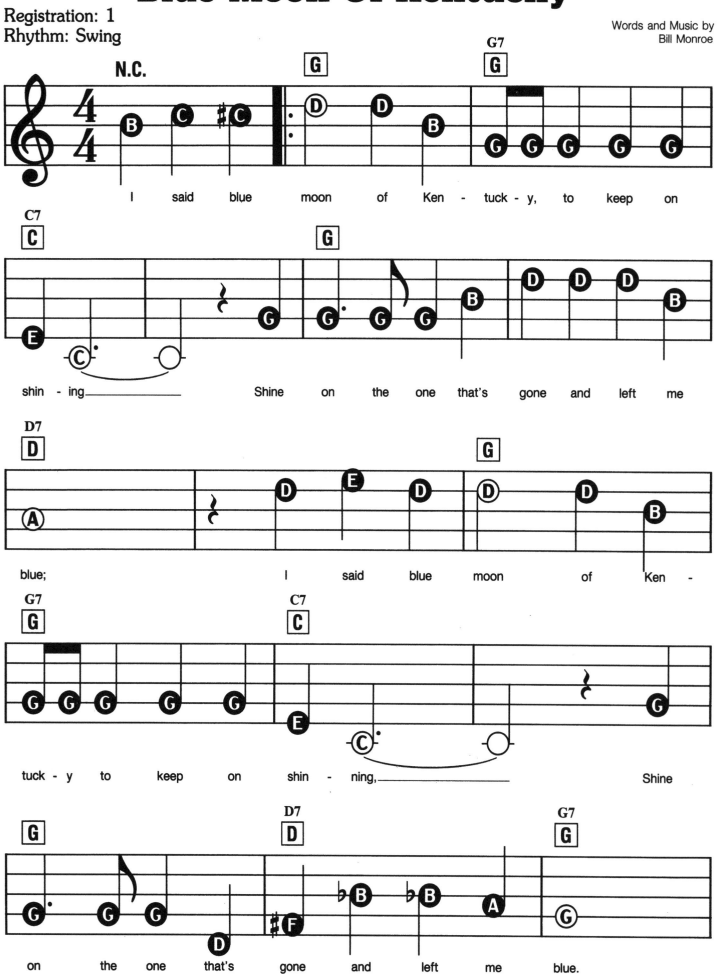

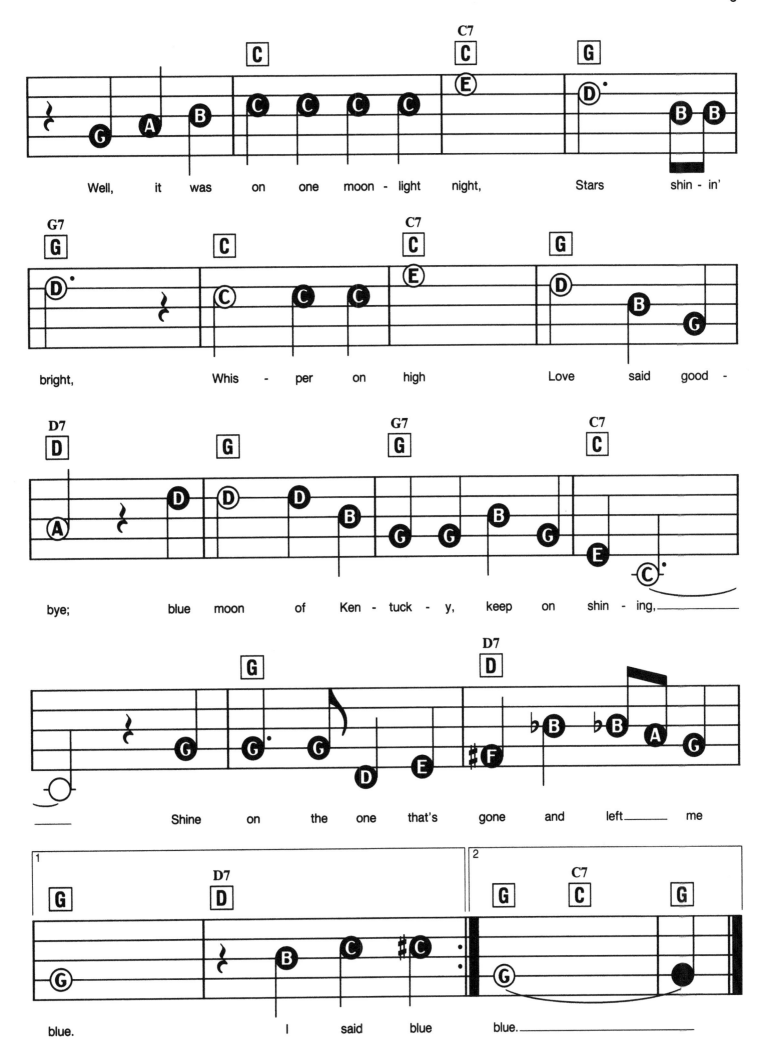

Crazy

Registration 2
Rhythm: Country or Swing

Words and Music by
Willie Nelson

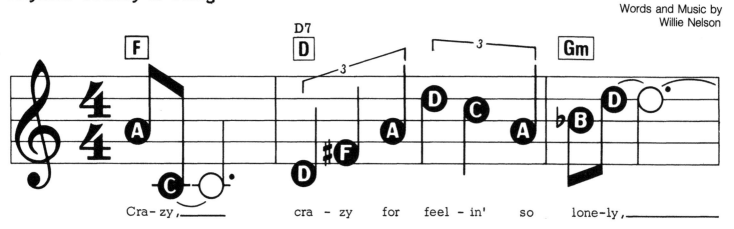

Cra-zy,____ cra-zy for feel-in' so lone-ly,____

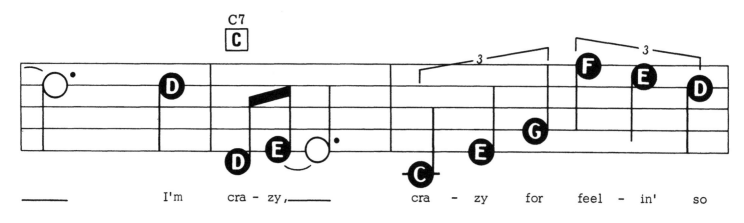

____ I'm cra-zy,____ cra-zy for feel-in' so

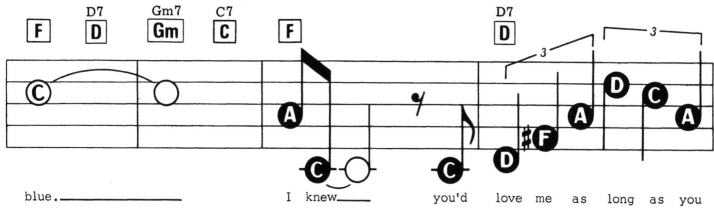

blue.____ I knew____ you'd love me as long as you

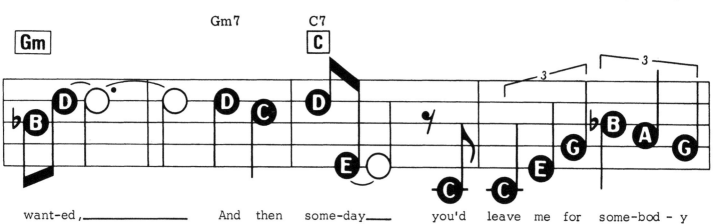

want-ed,____ And then some-day____ you'd leave me for some-bod-y

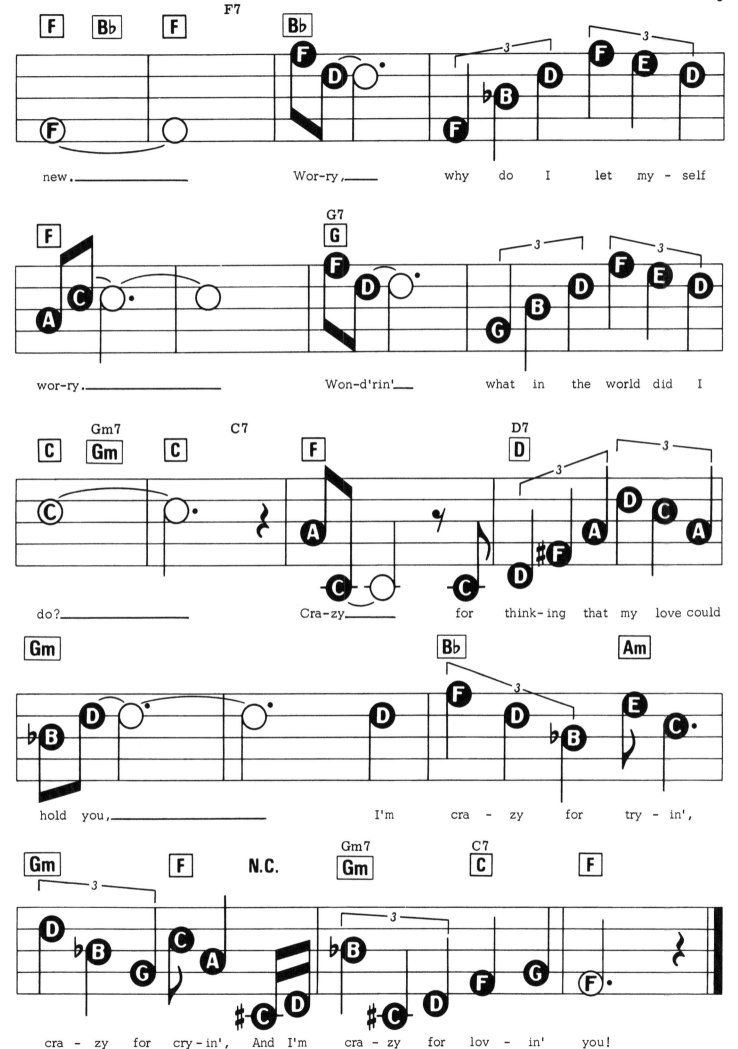

Back In Baby's Arms

Registration 4
Rhythm: Country, Fox-Trot, or Polka

Words and Music by
Bob Montgomery

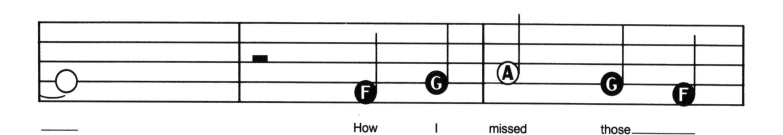

I'm   back   in_____   ba - by's   arms._____

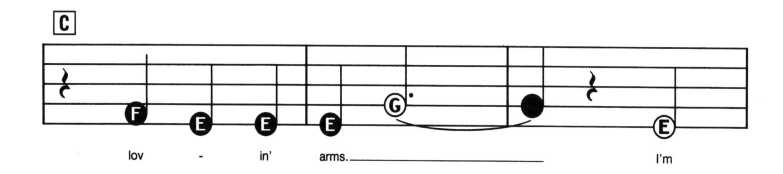

_____   How   I   missed   those_____

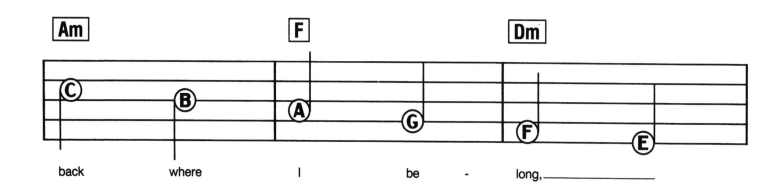

lov - in'   arms._____   I'm

back   where   I   be - long,_____

7

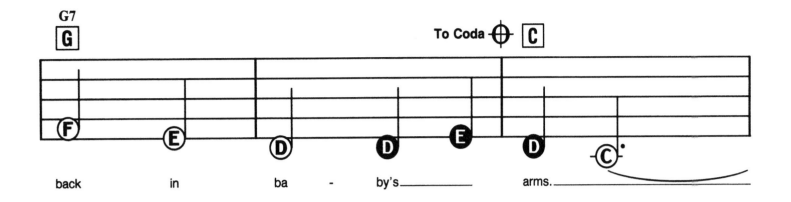

back in ba - by's _____ arms. _____

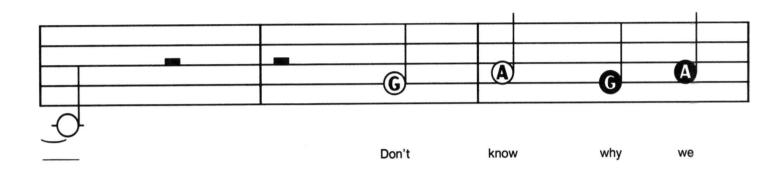

_____   Don't   know   why   we

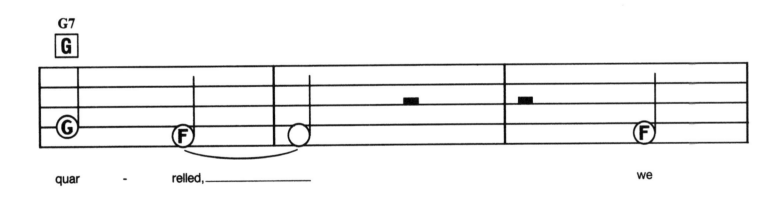

quar - relled, _____   we

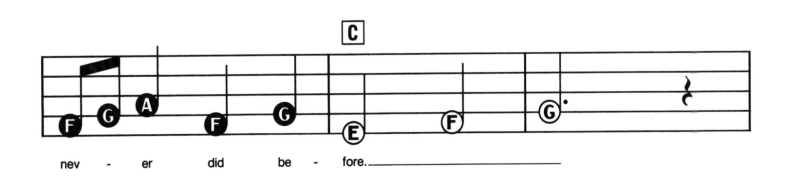

nev - er did be - fore. _____

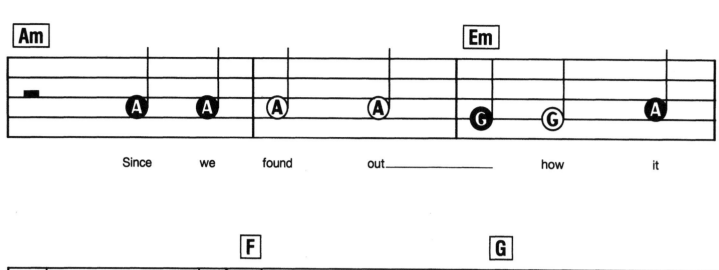

Since we found out_____ how it

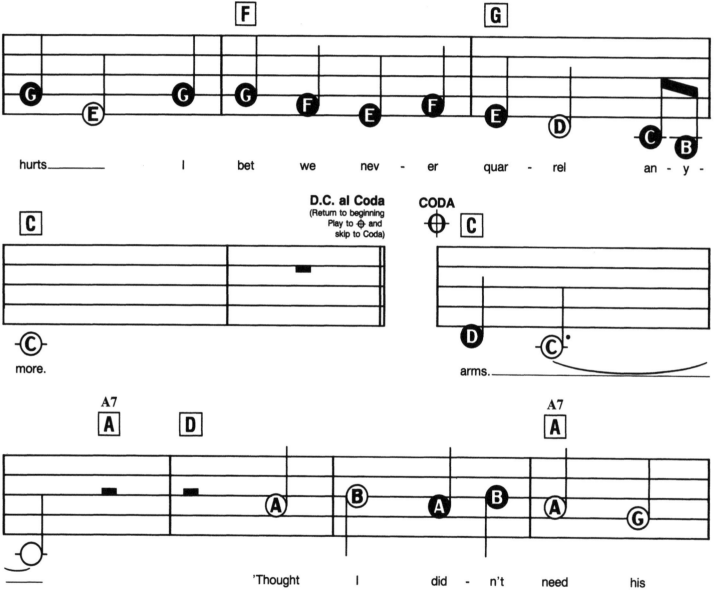

hurts_____ I bet we nev - er quar - rel an - y -

more.

arms._____

'Thought I did - n't need his

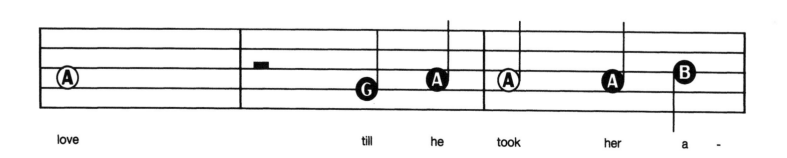

love till he took her a -

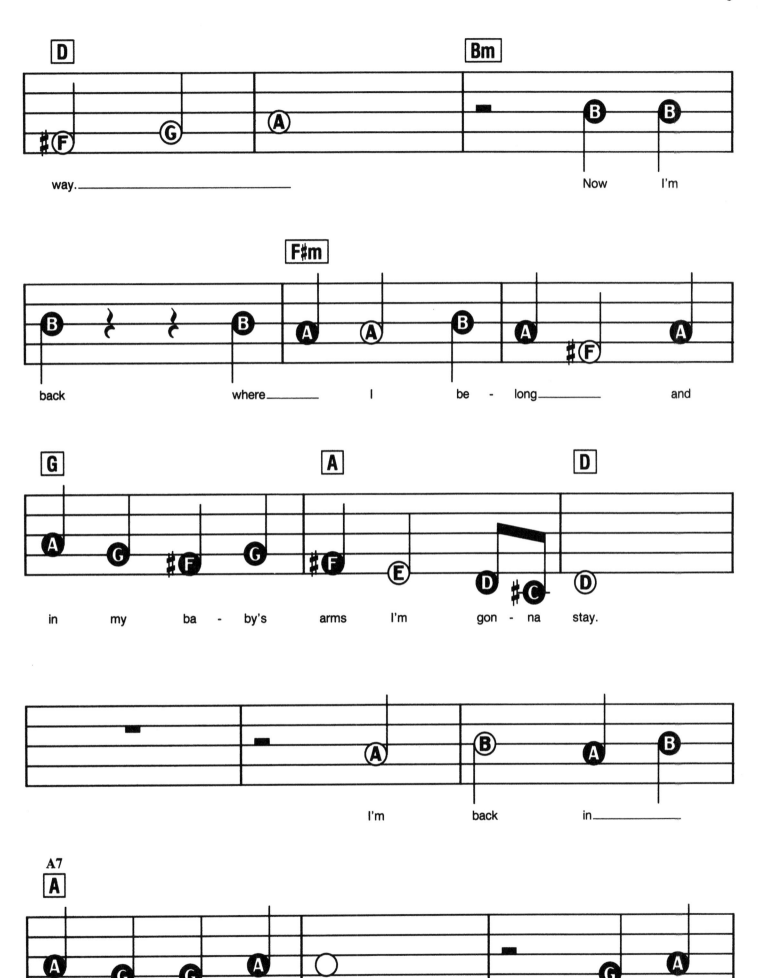

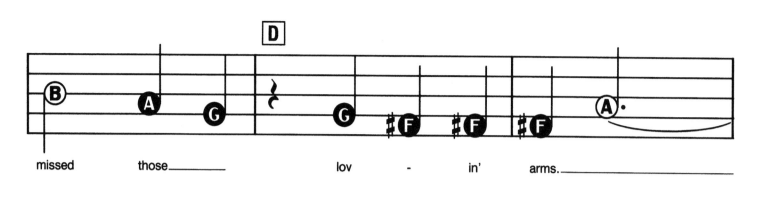

missed those_____ lov - in' arms._____

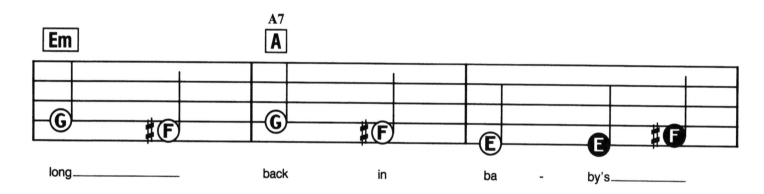

_____ I'm back where I be -

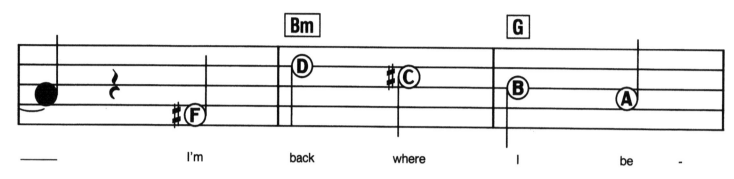

long_____ back in ba - by's_____

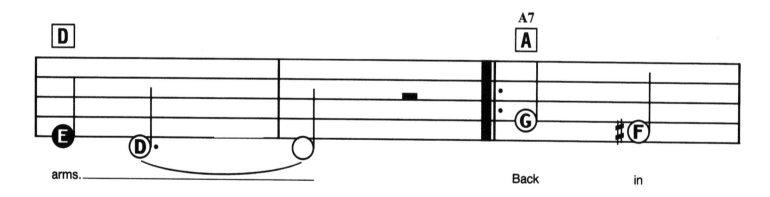

arms._____ Back in

Repeat and Fade

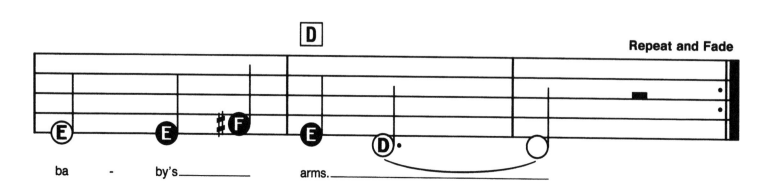

ba - by's_____ arms._____

Foolin' Round

Registration 7
Rhythm: Country, Fox-Trot, or Polka

Words and Music by
Harlan Howard and Buck Owens

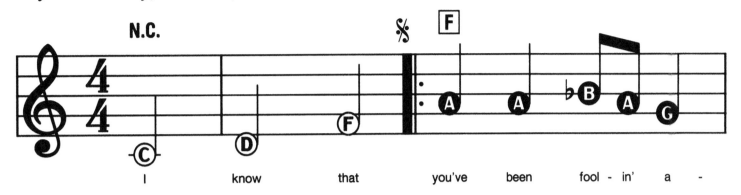

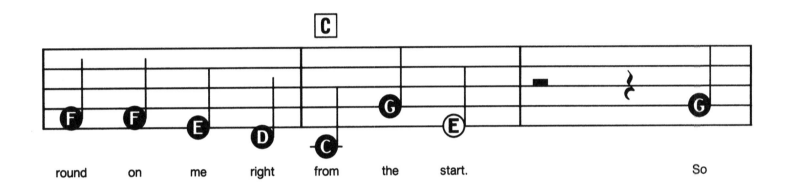

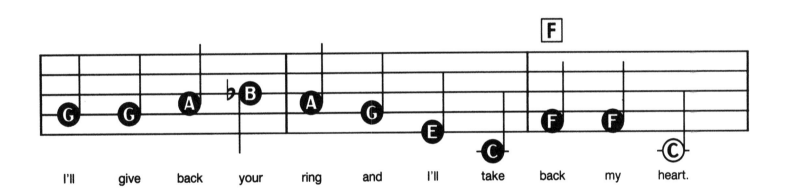

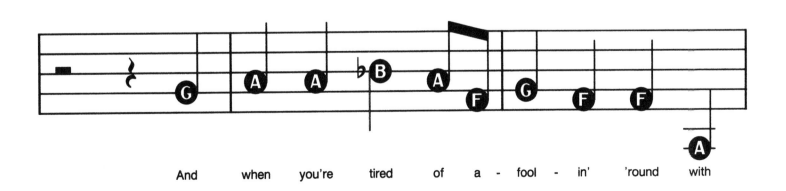

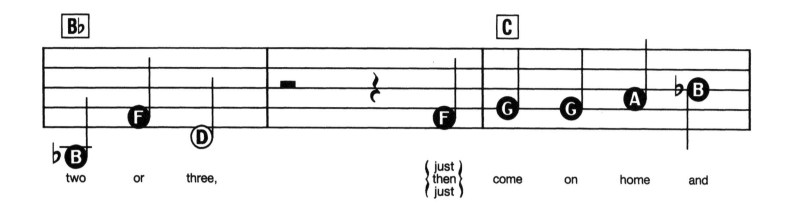

two　　or　　three,　　{just}{then}{just}　　come　　on　　home　　and

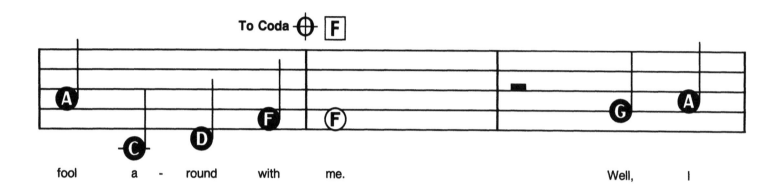

fool　　a　-　round　　with　　me.　　　　Well,　　I

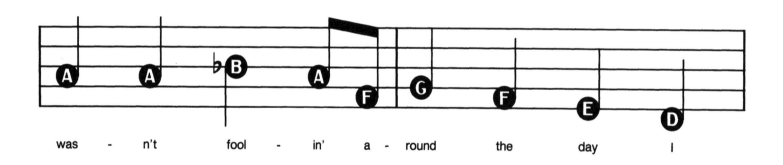

was　-　n't　　fool　-　in'　a　-　round　　the　　day　　I

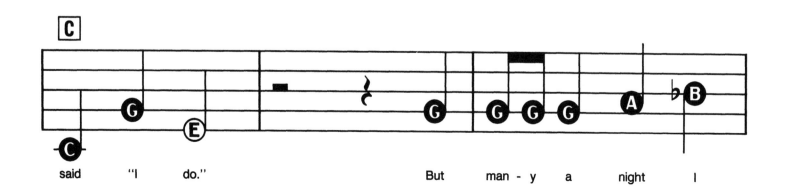

said　"I　do."　　　　But　man　-　y　　a　　night　　I

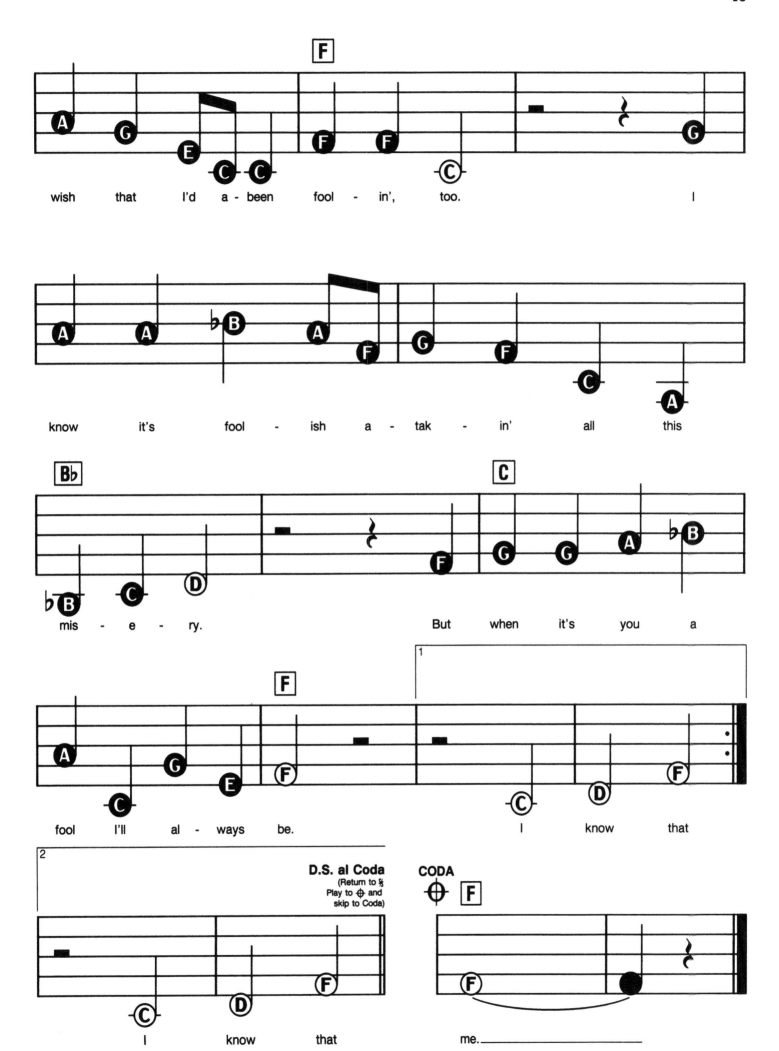

Faded Love

Registration 3
Rhythm: Country or Fox-Trot

Words and Music by
John Wills and Bob Wills

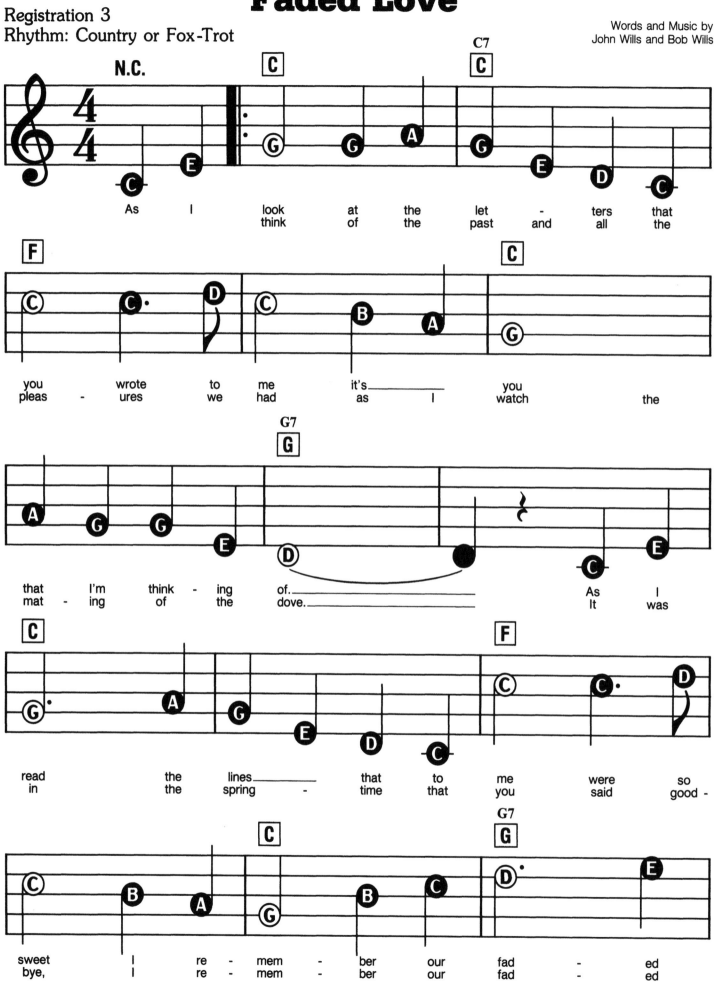

15

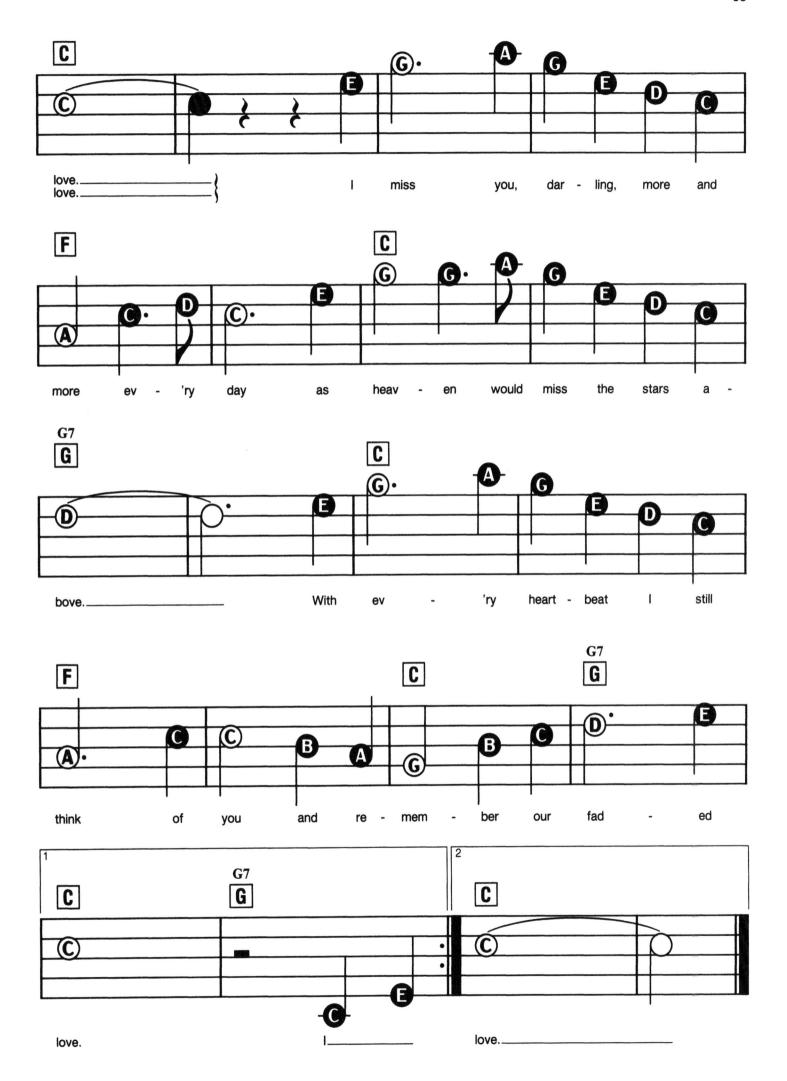

Have You Ever Been Lonely?
(Have You Ever Been Blue?)

Registration 3
Rhythm: Swing or Jazz

Words by George Brown
Music by Peter DeRose

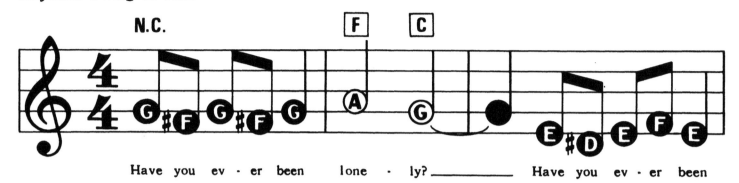

Have you ev-er been lone-ly? _____ Have you ev-er been

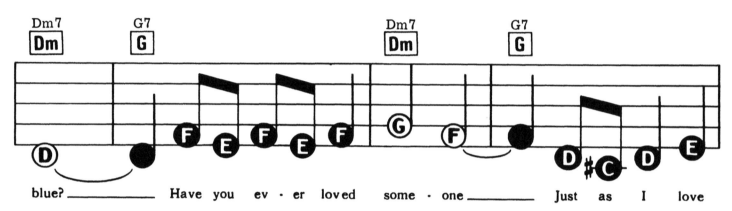

blue? _____ Have you ev-er loved some-one _____ Just as I love

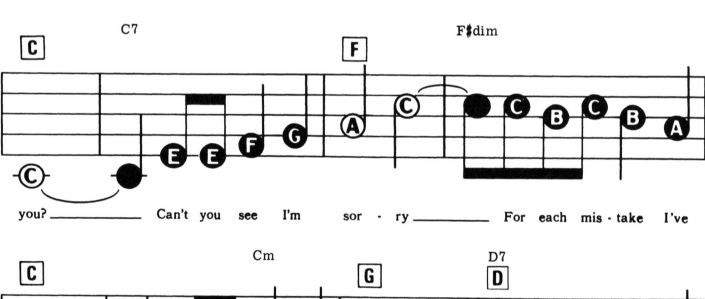

you? _____ Can't you see I'm sor-ry _____ For each mis-take I've

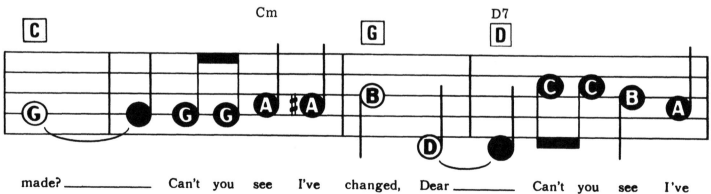

made? _____ Can't you see I've changed, Dear _____ Can't you see I've

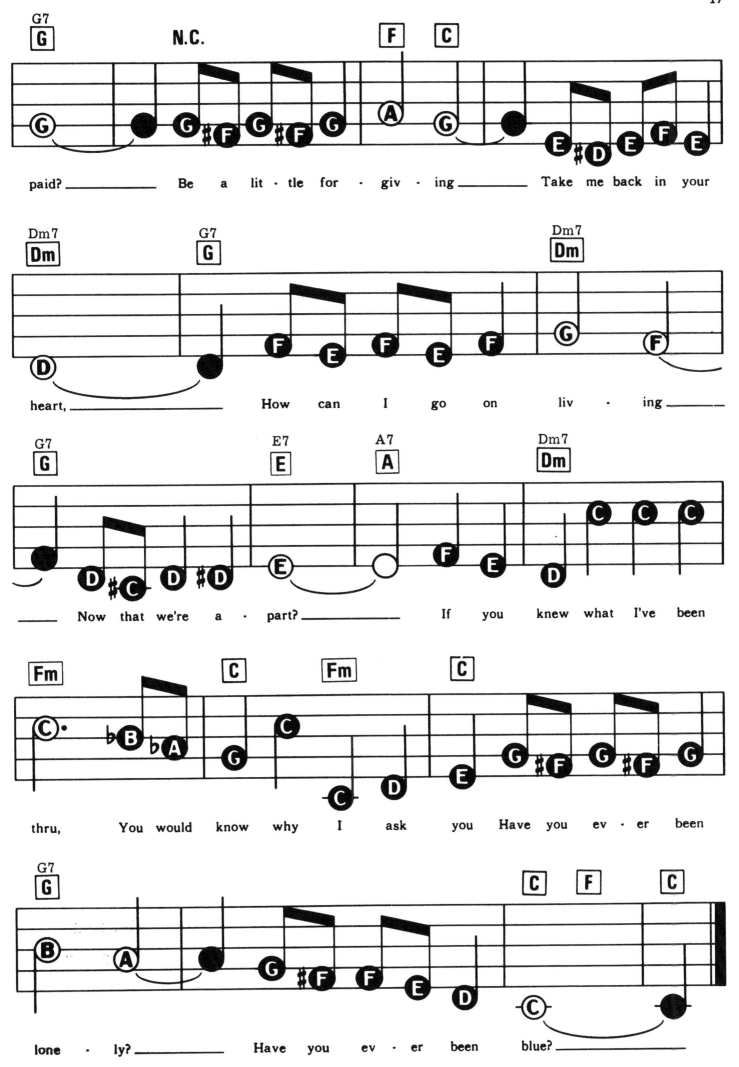

Heartaches

Registration 4
Rhythm: Fox Trot or Swing

Words by John Klenner
Music by Al Hoffman

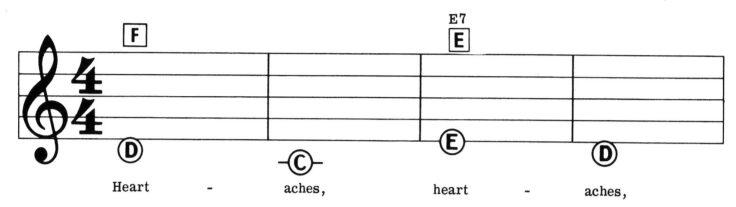

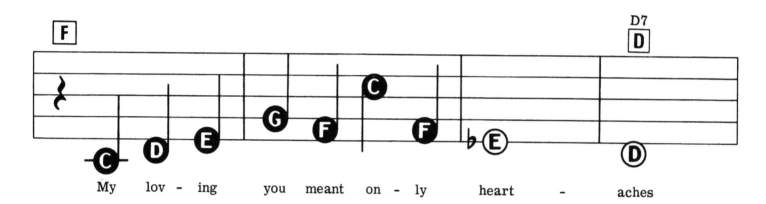

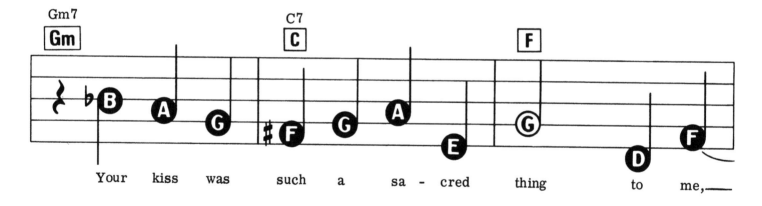

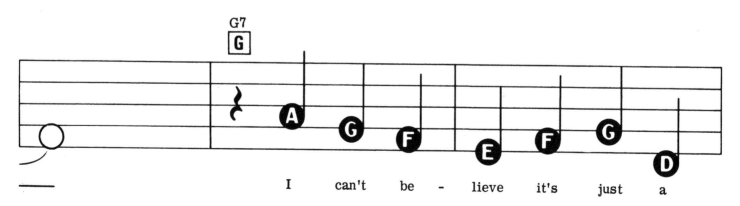

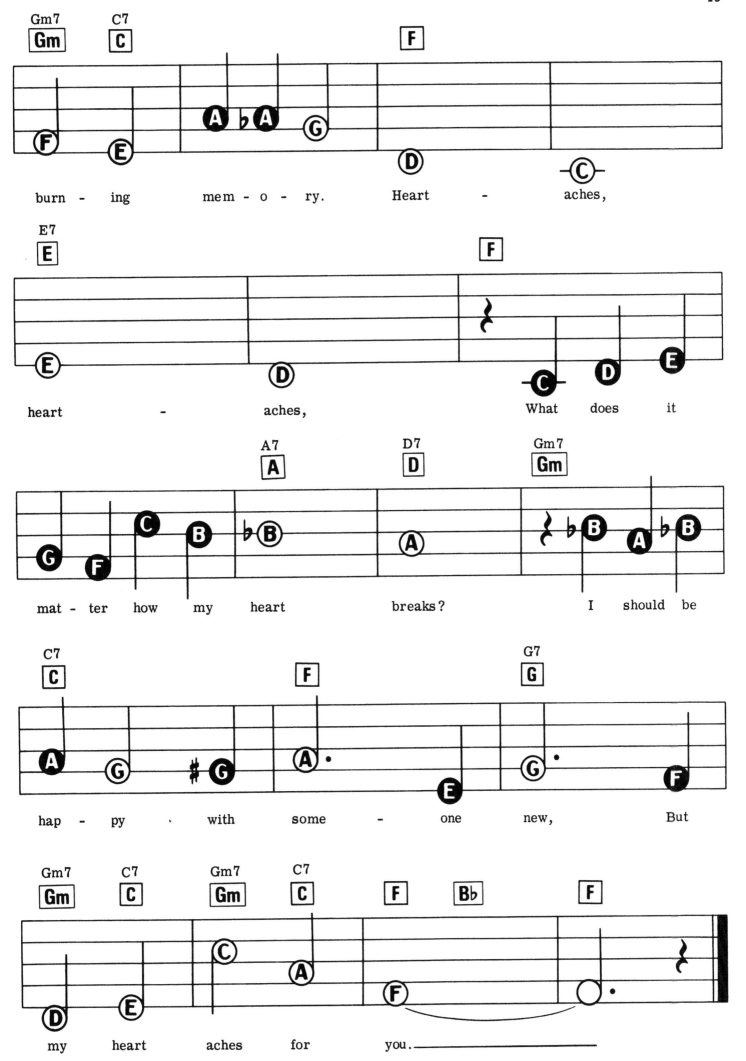

I Fall To Pieces

Registration 9
Rhythm: Country or Shuffle

Words and Music by
Hank Cochran and Harlan Howard

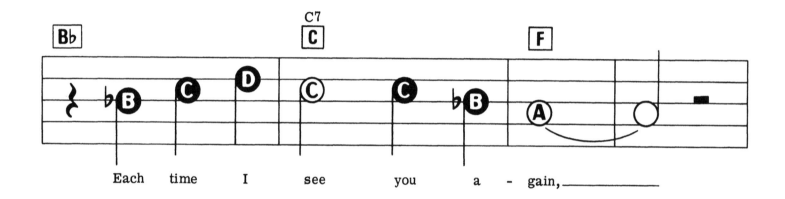

I fall ___ to piec - es ___

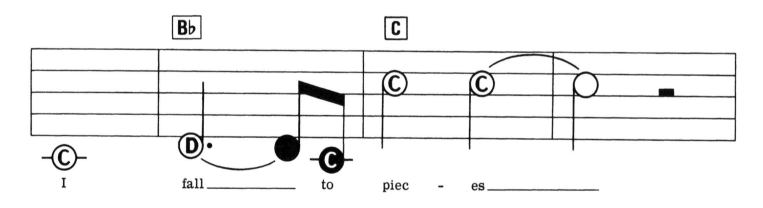

Each time I see you a - gain, ___

I fall ___ to piec - es ___

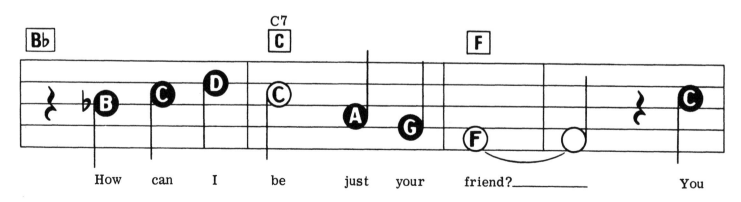

How can I be just your friend? ___ You

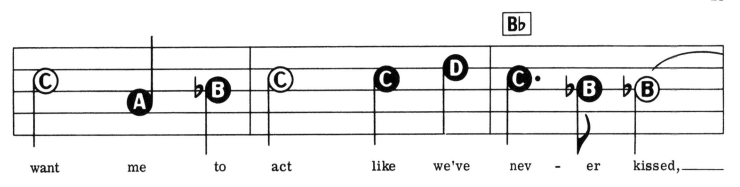

want me to act like we've nev - er kissed,_____

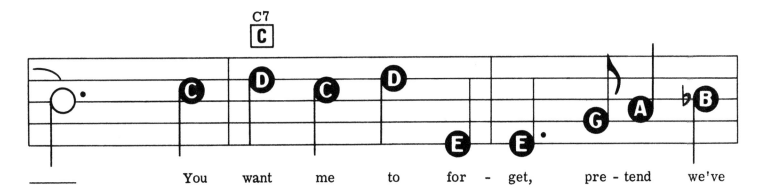

_____ You want me to for - get, pre - tend we've

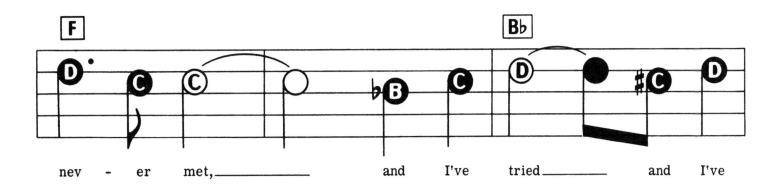

nev - er met,_____ and I've tried_____ and I've

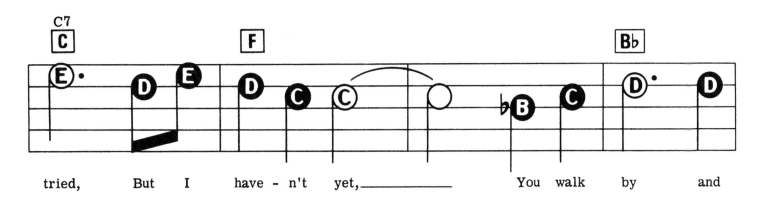

tried, But I have - n't yet,_____ You walk by and

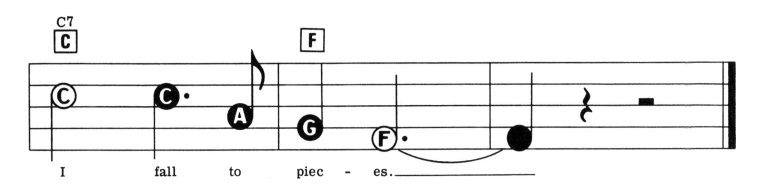

I fall to piec - es._____

Leavin' On Your Mind

Registration 9
Rhythm: Ballad

Words and Music by
Wayne P. Walker and Webb Pierce

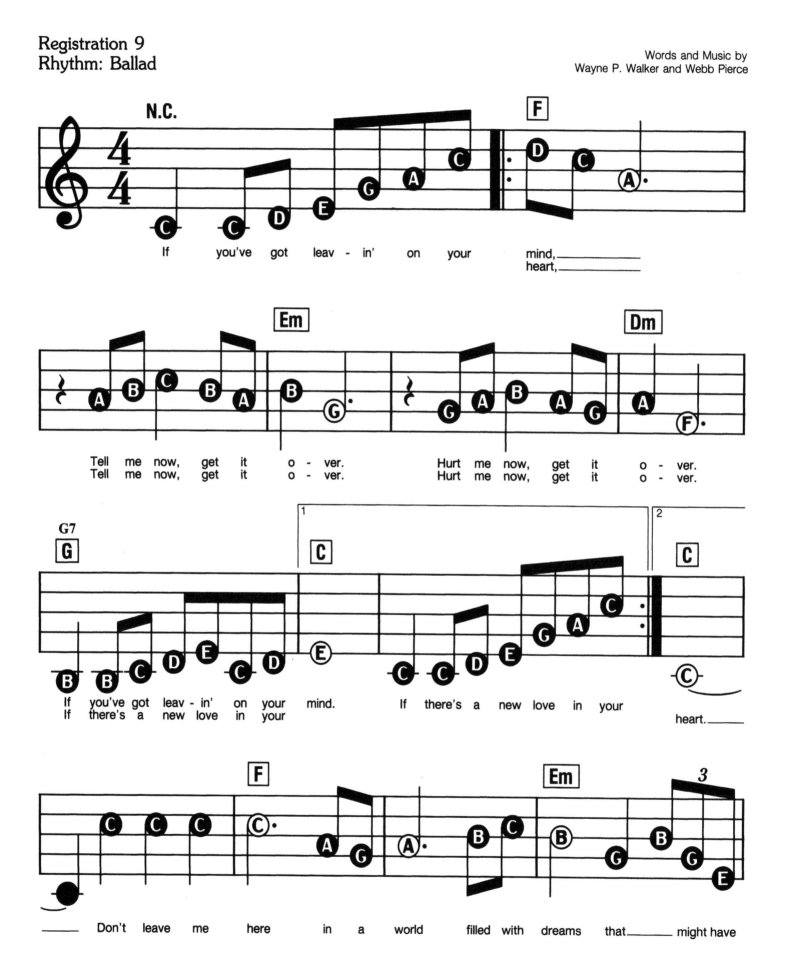

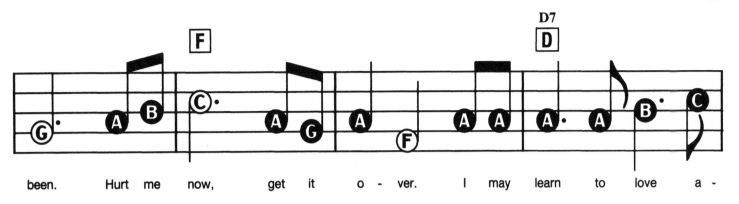

been. Hurt me now, get it o - ver. I may learn to love a -

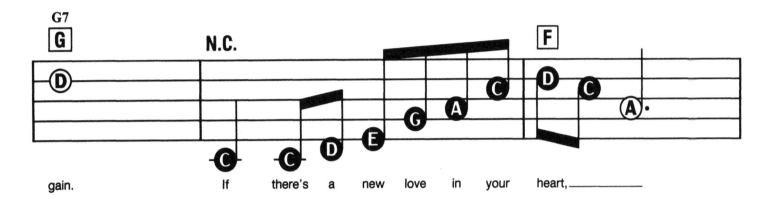

gain. If there's a new love in your heart,_____

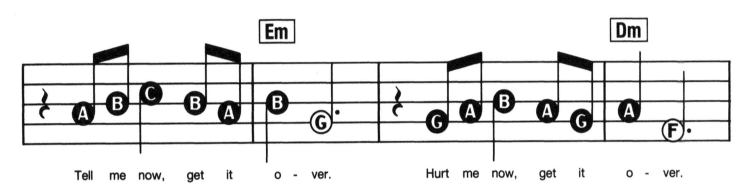

Tell me now, get it o - ver. Hurt me now, get it o - ver.

If there's a new love in your heart._____ Hurt me now, get it

o - ver. If there's a new love in your heart._____

Loose Talk

Registration 5
Rhythm: Country, Fox-Trot, or Polka

Words and Music by
Freddie Hart and Ann Lucas

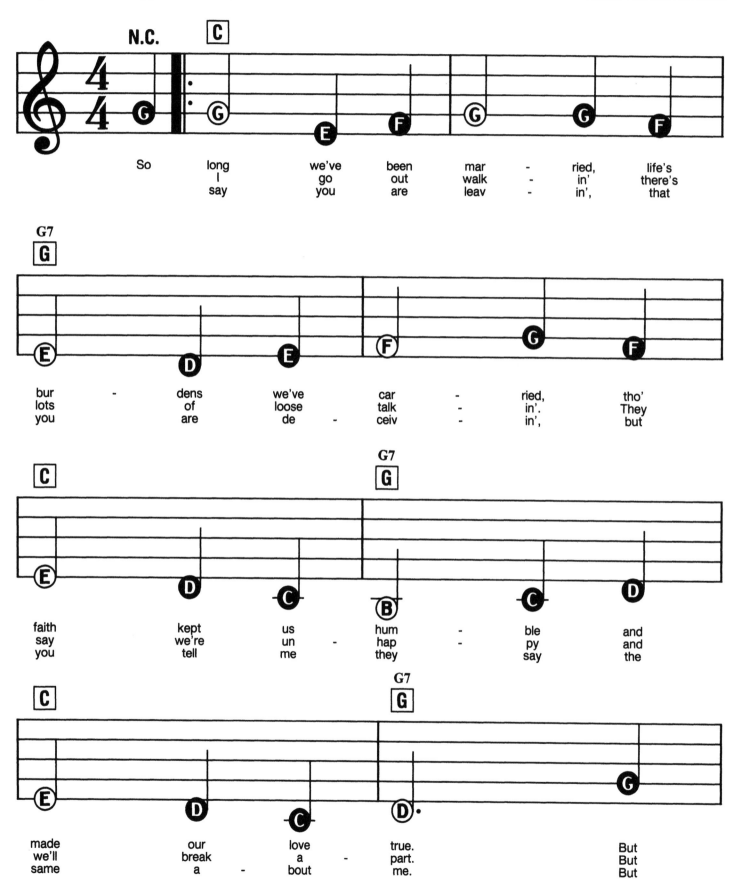

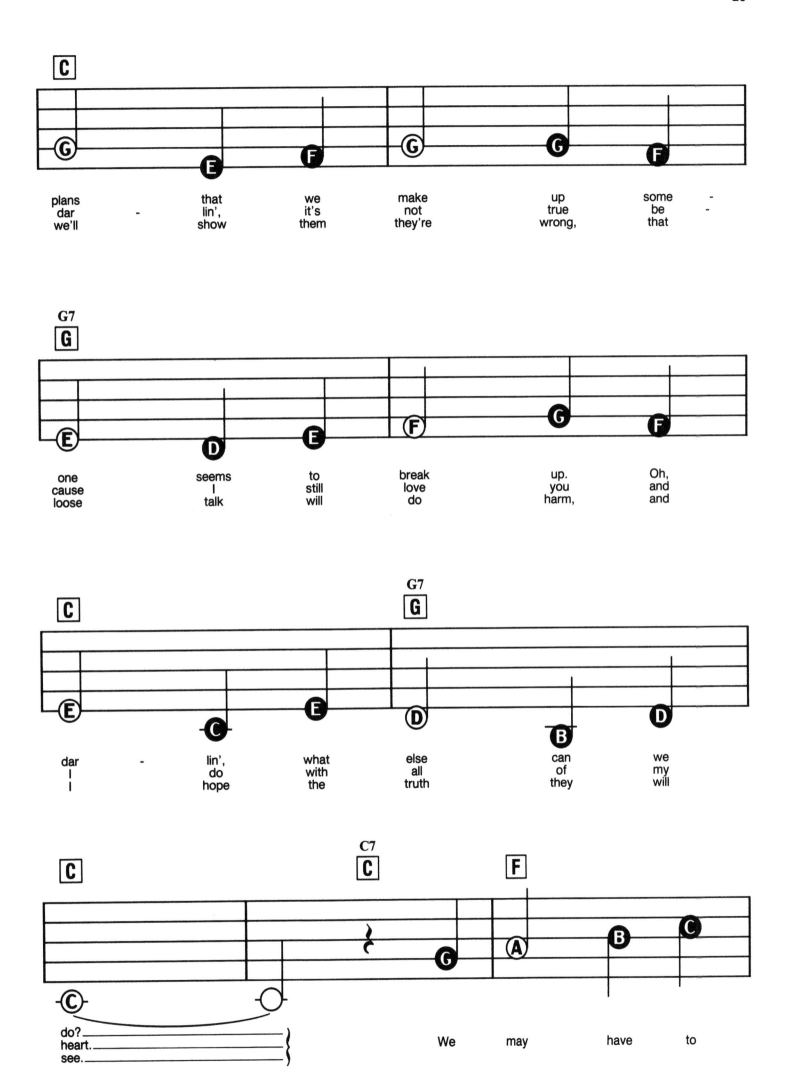

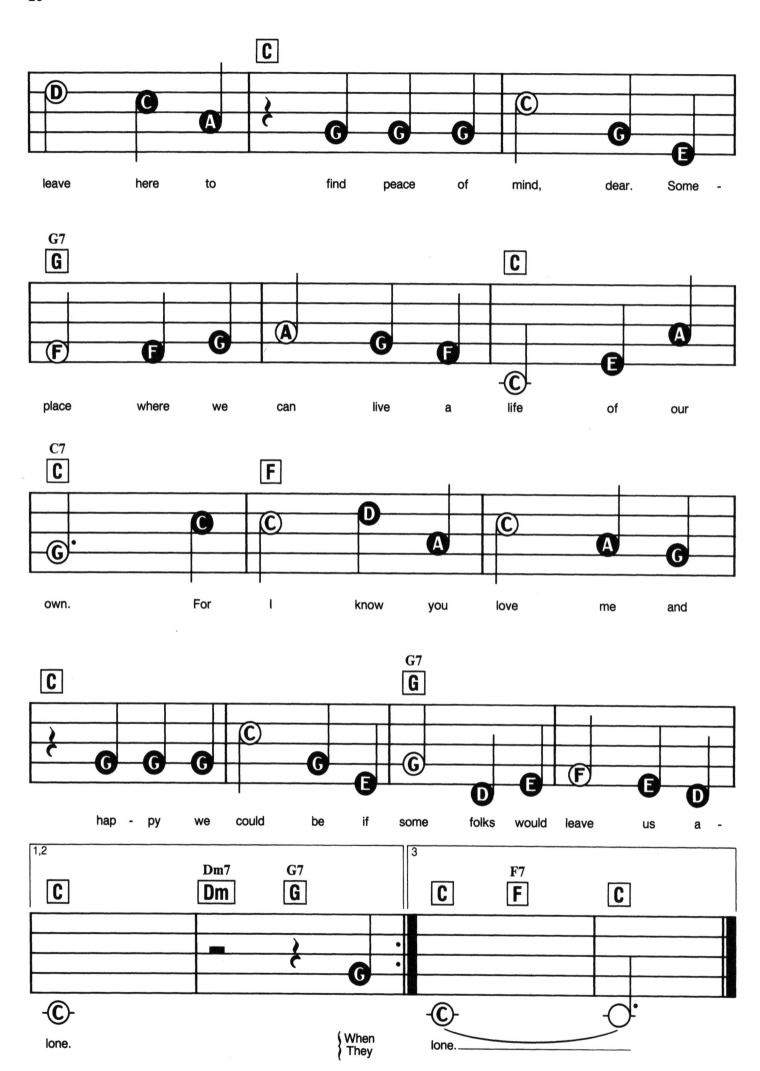

San Antonio Rose

Registration 8
Rhythm: Country Western or Fox-Trot

Words and Music by
Bob Wills

Deep with - in my heart lies a mel - o - dy, A song of old San An - tone_____ Where in dreams I live with a mem - o - ry, Be - neath the stars all a - lone._____ It was there I found be - side the Al - a - mo, En - chant - ment strange as the

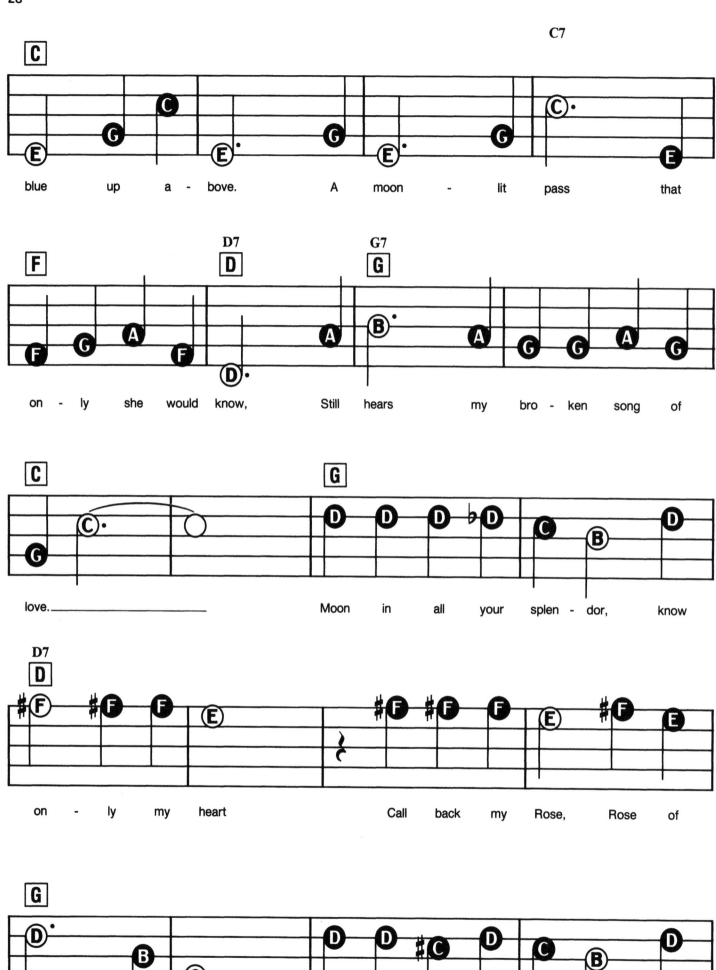

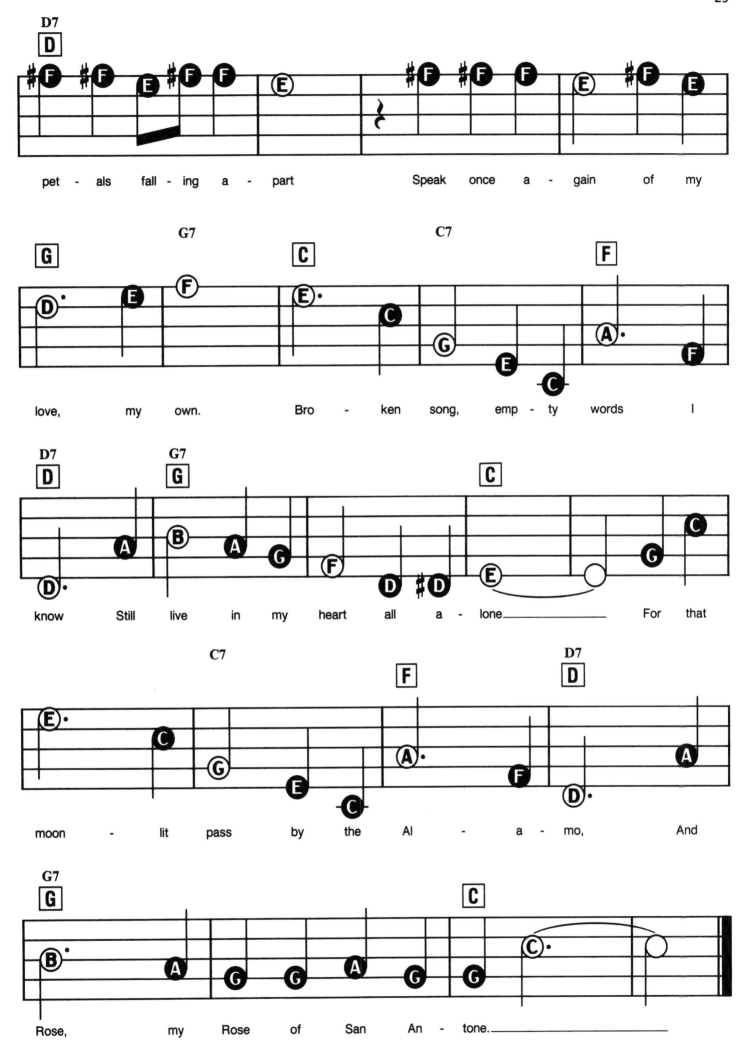

Seven Lonely Days

Registration 2
Rhythm: Country, Fox-Trot, or Pops

By Earl Shuman,
Alden Shuman and Marshall Brown

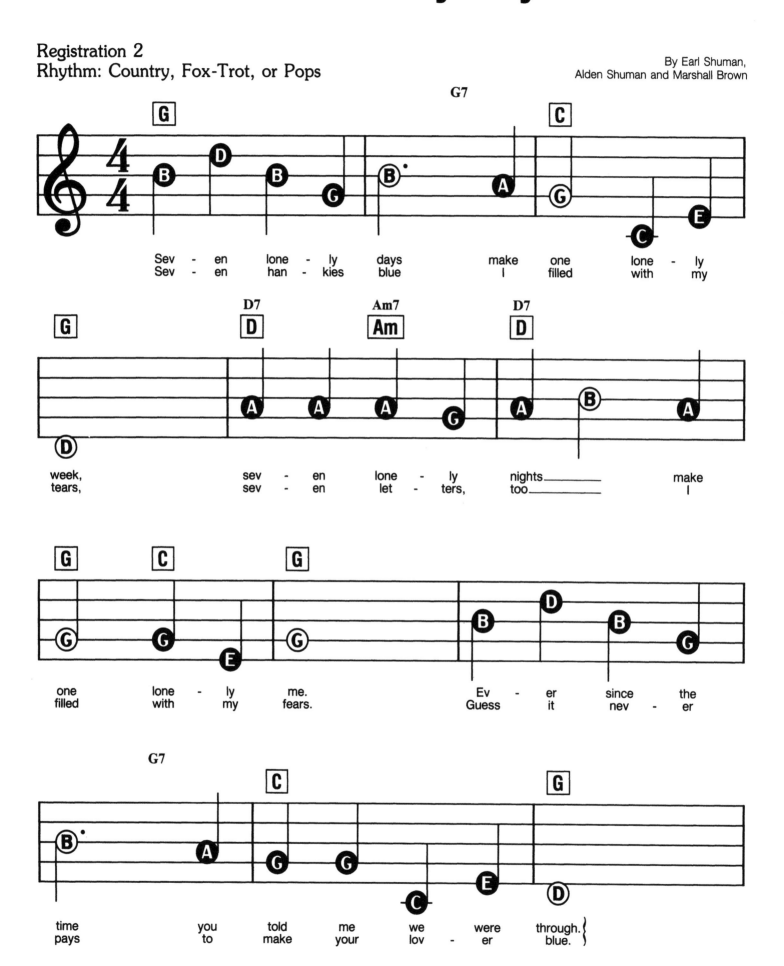

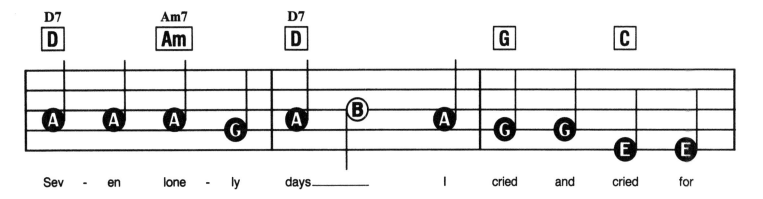

Sev - en lone - ly days_____ I cried and cried for

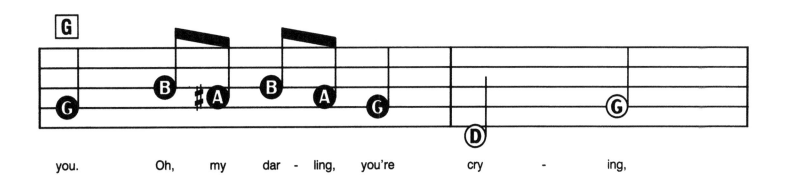

you. Oh, my dar - ling, you're cry - ing,

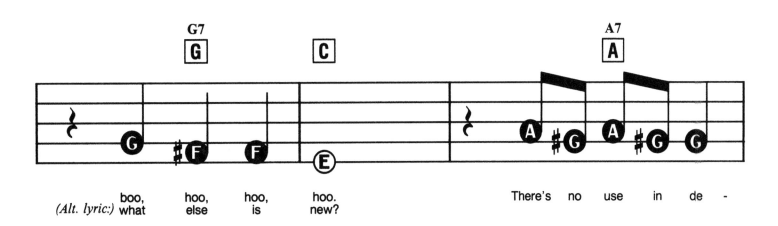

(Alt. lyric:) boo, hoo, hoo, hoo.
what else is new?

There's no use in de -

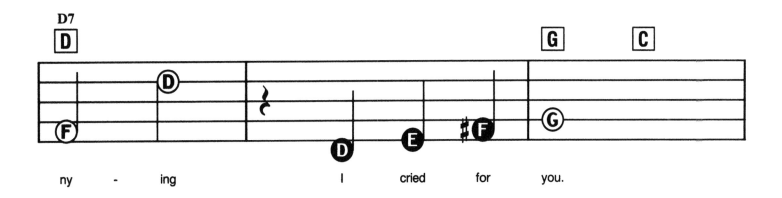

ny - ing I cried for you.

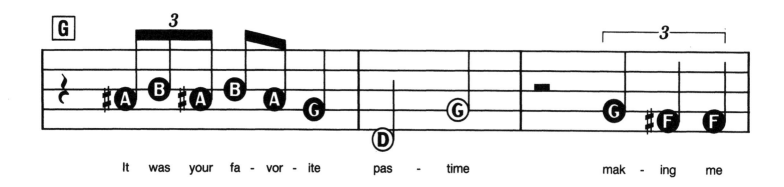

It was your fa - vor - ite pas - time mak - ing me

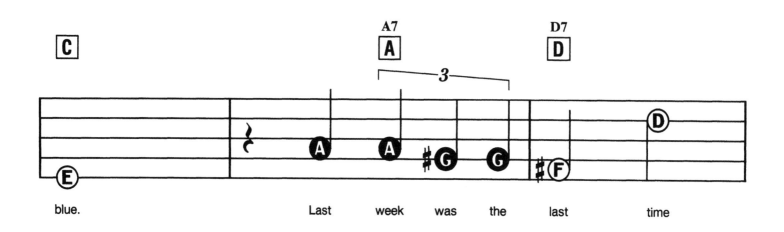

blue. Last week was the last time

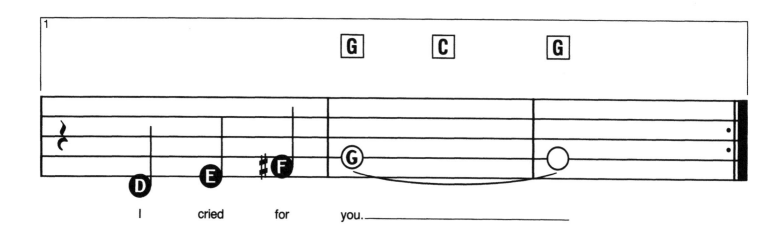

I cried for you.

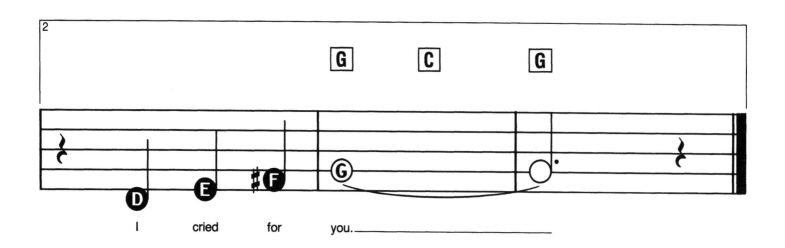

I cried for you.

So Wrong

Registration 8
Rhythm: Pops, Rock, or Country

Words and Music by Carl Perkins,
Mel Tillis and Danny Dill

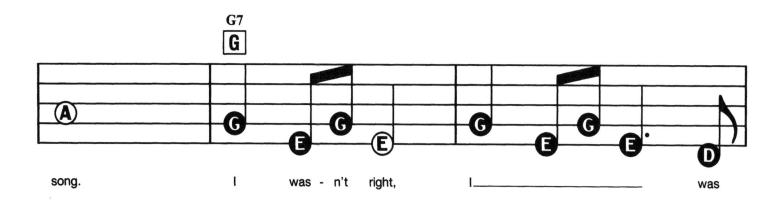

song.   I was - n't right, I_____ was

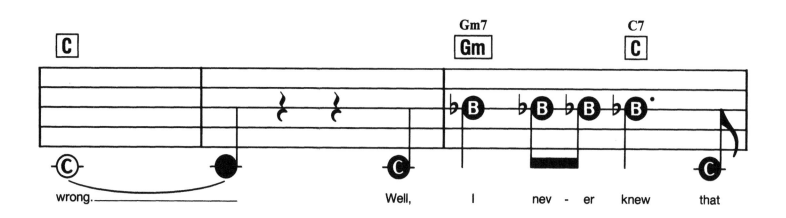

wrong._____   Well, I nev - er knew that

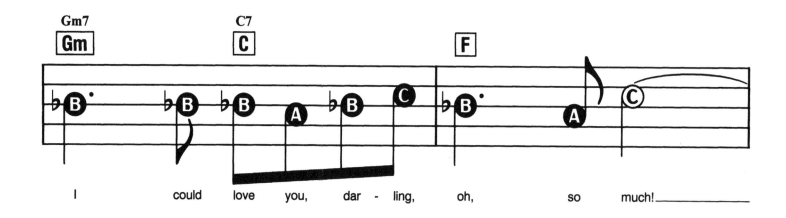

I could love you, dar - ling, oh, so much!_____

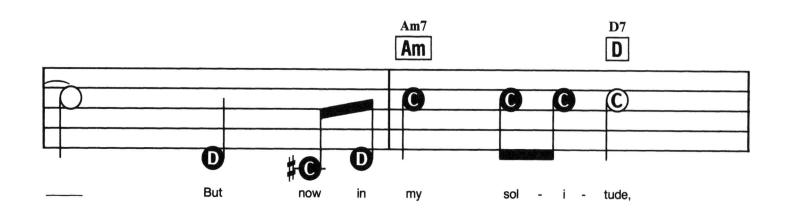

_____ But now in my sol - i - tude,

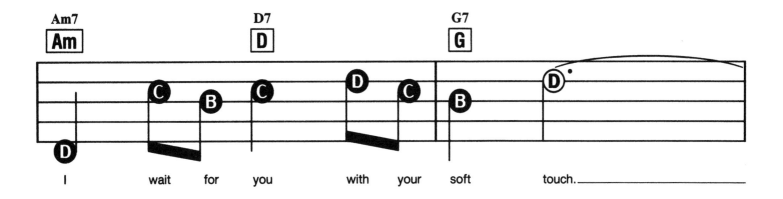

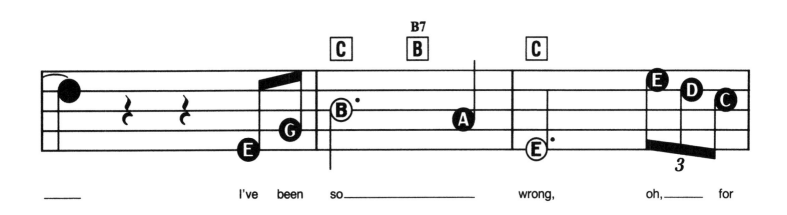

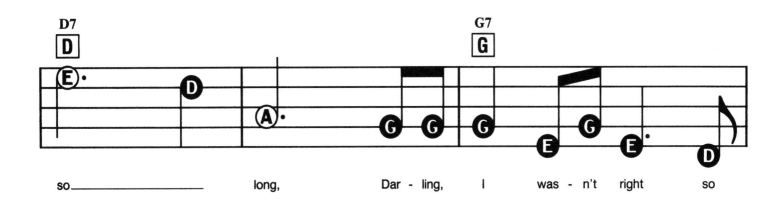

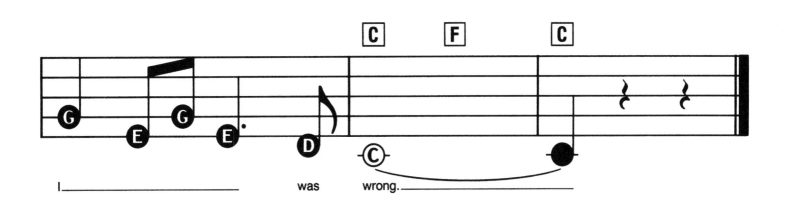

She's Got You

Registration 10
Rhythm: Country or Pops

Words and Music by
Hank Cochran

I've got your pic - ture____ That you gave to me and____ it's
rec - ords____ That we used to share and they still

signed "with love" just like it used to be.____ The on - ly thing
sound the same as when you were here.____ The on - ly thing

dif - f'rent,____ the on - ly thing new, I've got your
dif - f'rent,____ the on - ly thing new, I've got the

pic - ture,____ She's got you. I've got the
rec - ords,____ She's got

you. I've got your

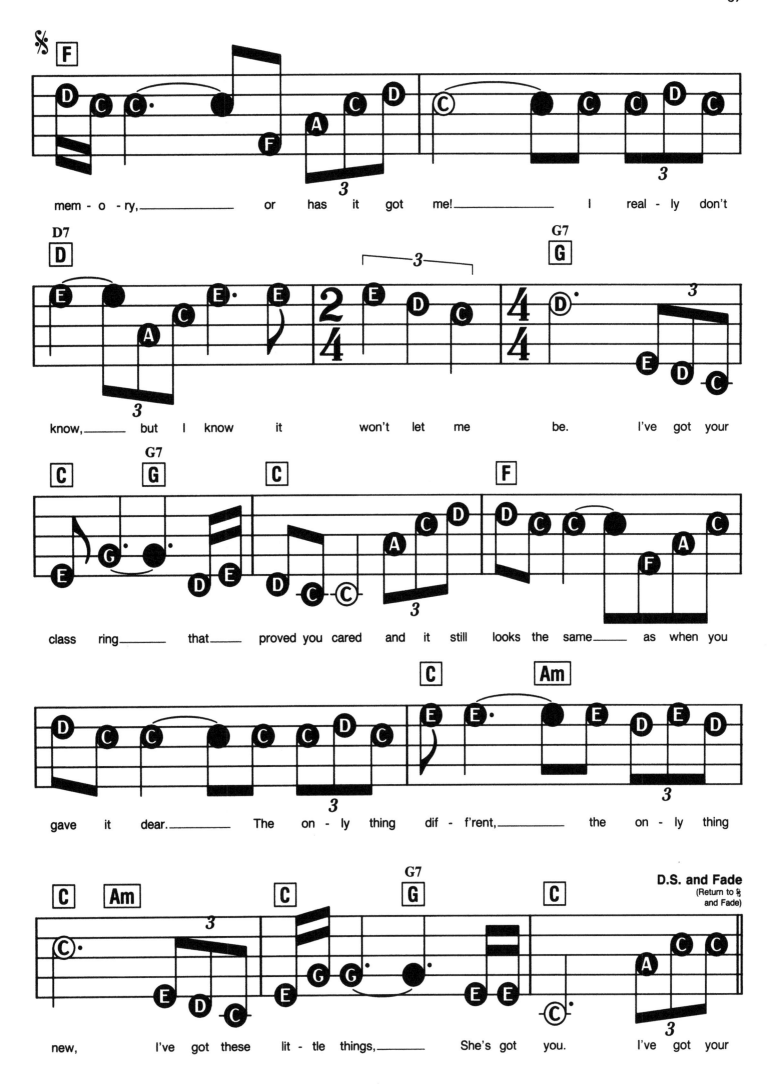

Sweet Dreams

Registration 5
Rhythm: Country, Fox-Trot, or Pops

By Don Gibson

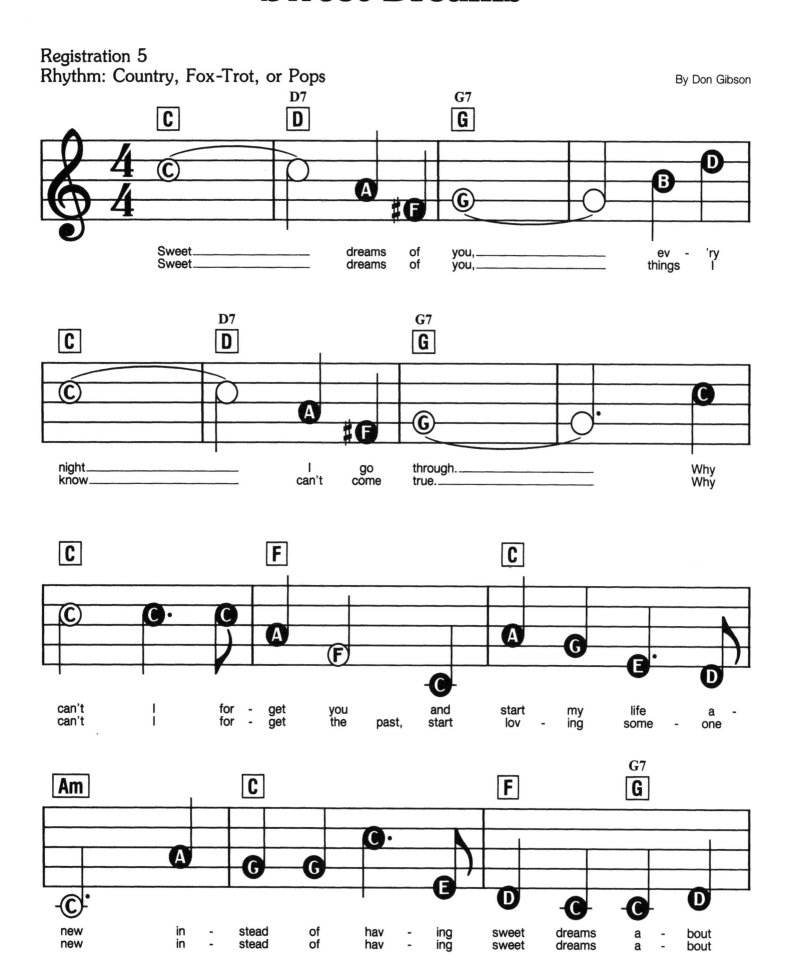

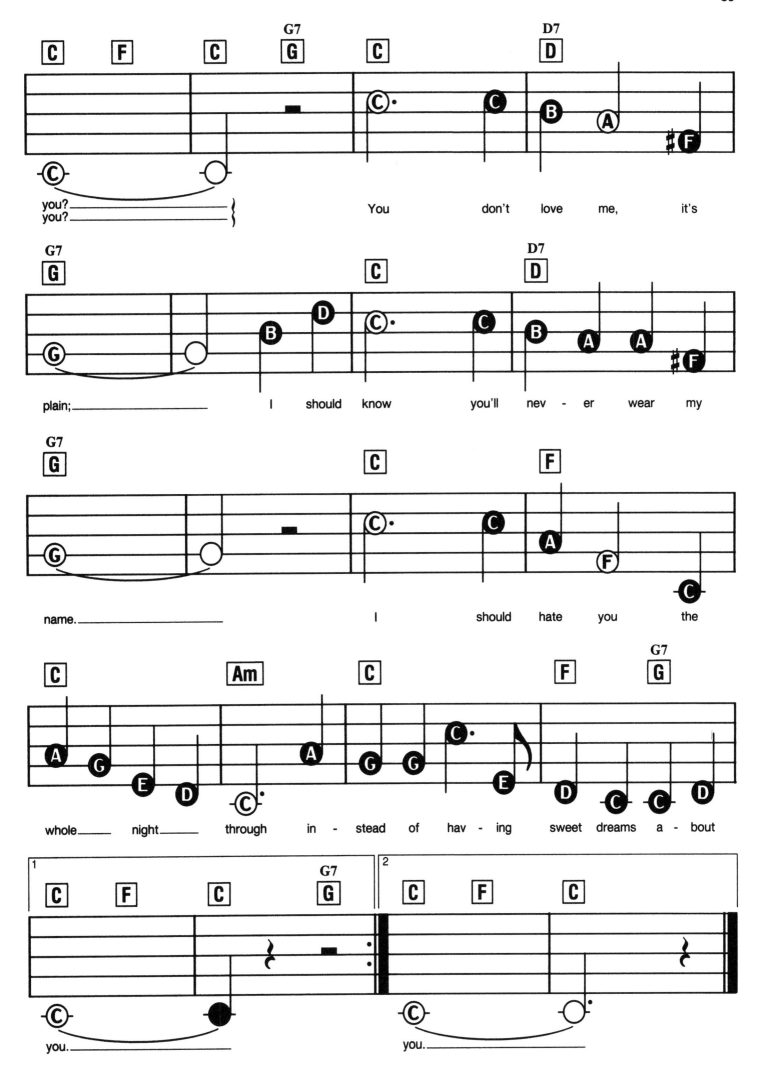

Strange

Registration 3
Rhythm: Bossa Nova, Rhumba, or Pops

Words and Music by
Mel Tillis and Fred Burch

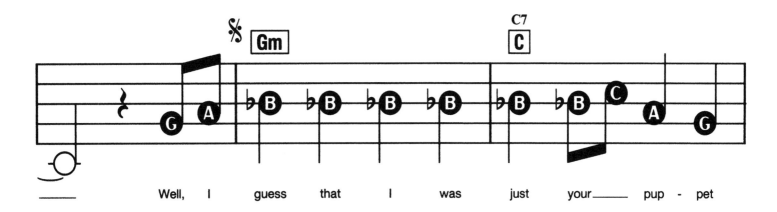

Well, I guess that I was just your_____ pup - pet

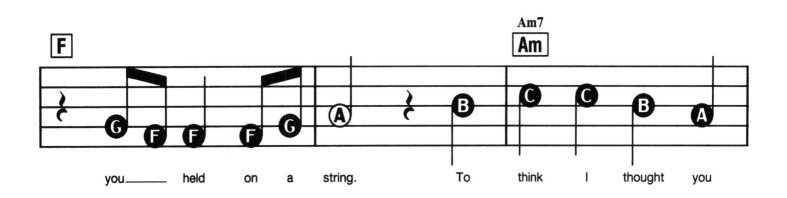

you_____ held on a string. To think I thought you

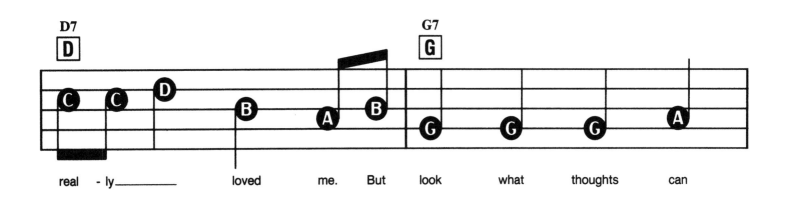

real - ly_____ loved me. But look what thoughts can

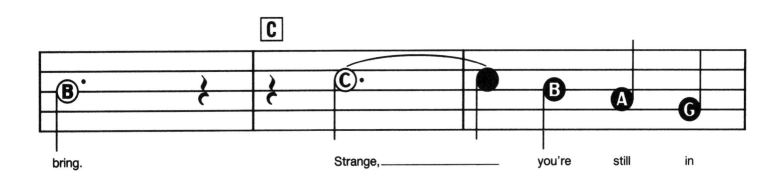

bring. Strange,_____ you're still in

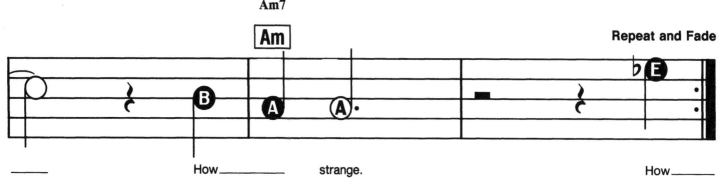

There He Goes

Registration 7
Rhythm: Swing, Fox-Trot, or Pops

Words and Music by Eddie Miller,
Durwood Haddock and W.S. Stevenson

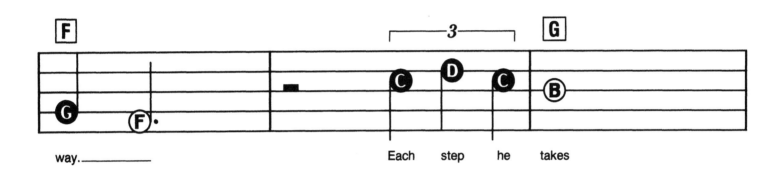

There____ he____ goes.   He's walk - ing a -

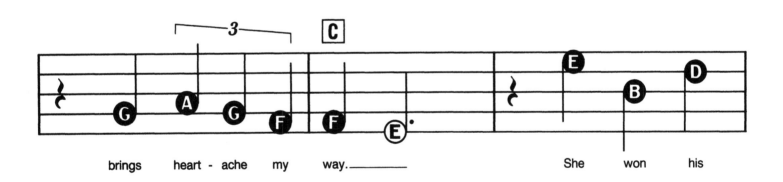

way.____   Each step he takes   brings heart - ache my way.____   She won his

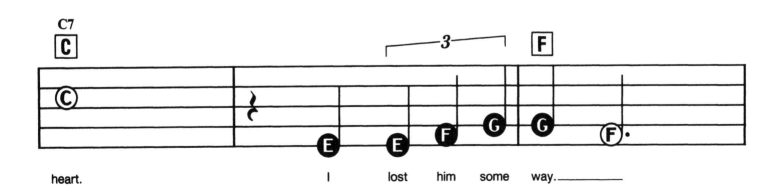

heart.   I lost him some way.____

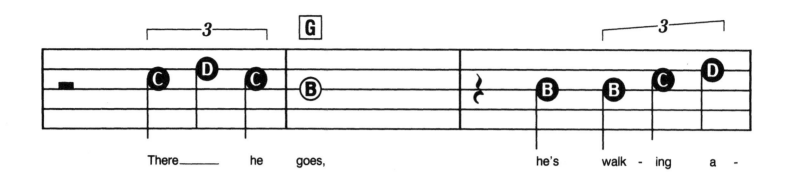

There___ he goes, he's walk - ing a -

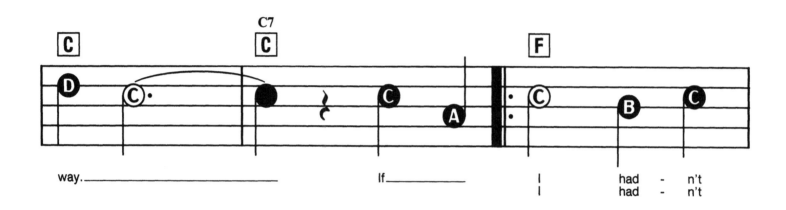

way.___ If___ I had - n't
I had - n't

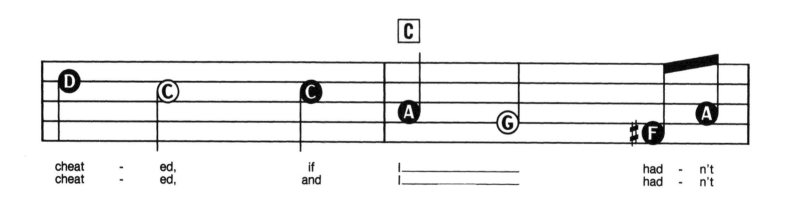

cheat - ed, if I___ had - n't
cheat - ed, and I___ had - n't

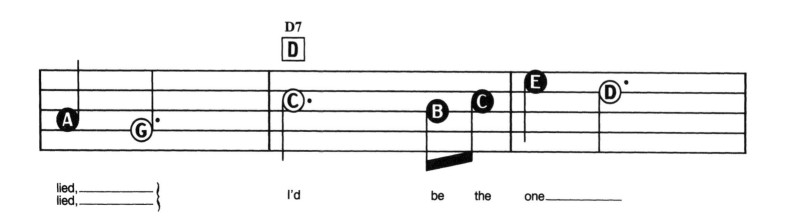

lied,___ I'd be the one___
lied,___

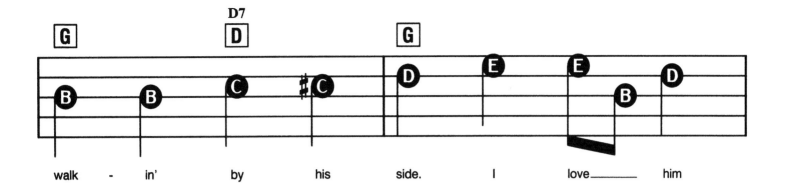

walk - in' by his side. I love_____ him

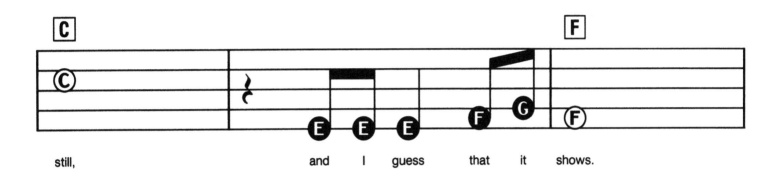

still, and I guess that it shows.

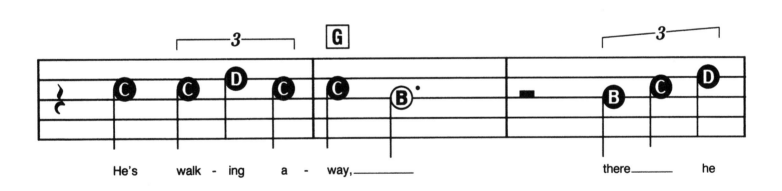

He's walk - ing a - way,_____ there_____ he

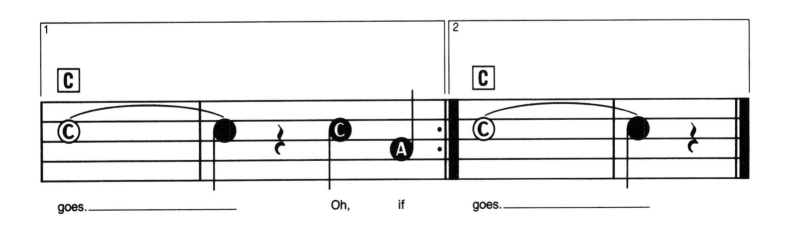

goes._____ Oh, if goes._____

Three Cigarettes In An Ashtray

Registration 3
Rhythm: Waltz

Words and Music by
Eddie Miller and W.S. Stevenson

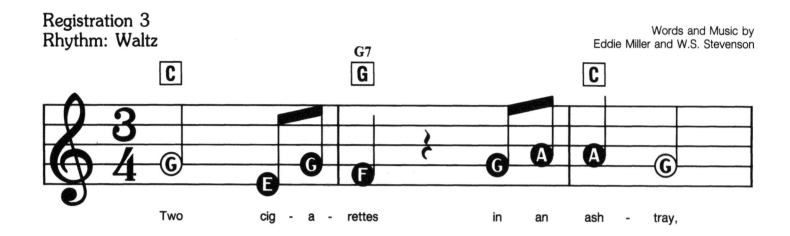

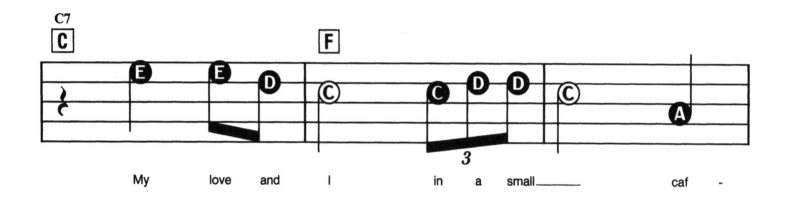

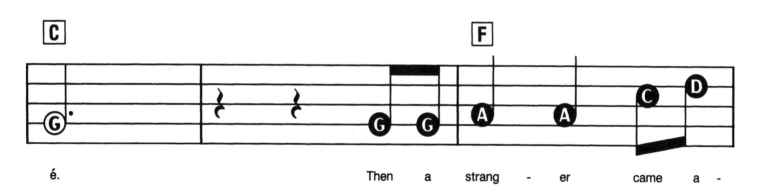

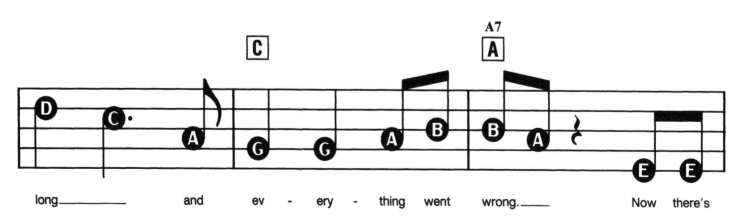

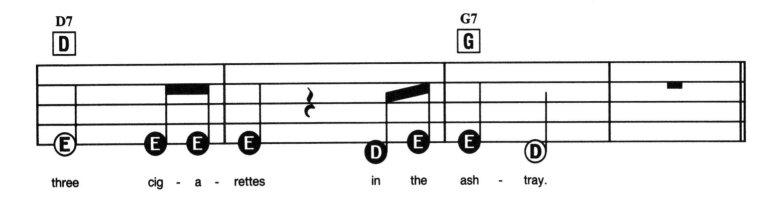

three cig - a - rettes in the ash - tray.

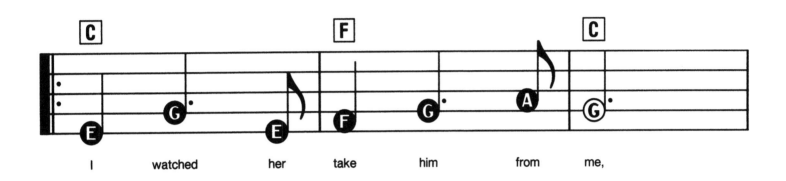

I watched her take him from me,

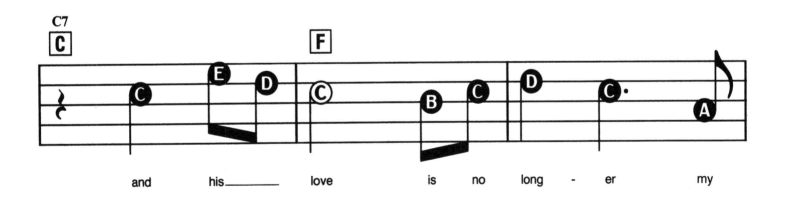

and his_____ love is no long - er my

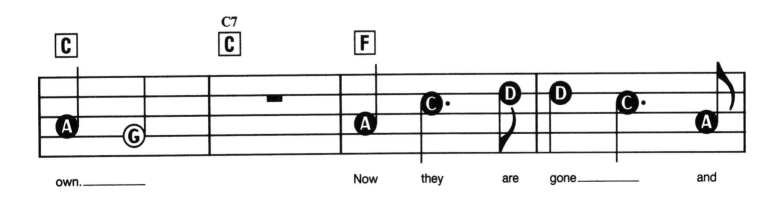

own._____ Now they are gone_____ and

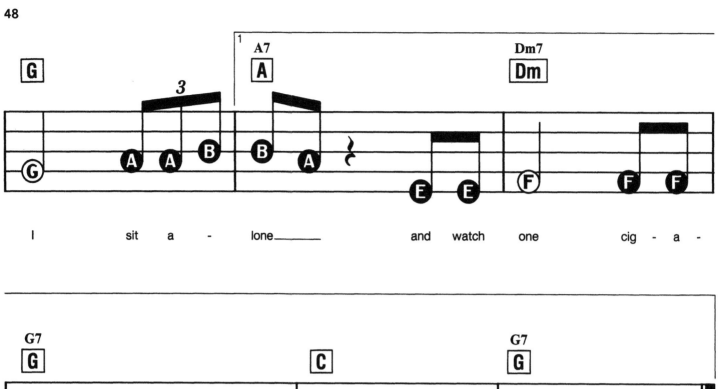

I sit a - lone_____ and watch one cig - a -

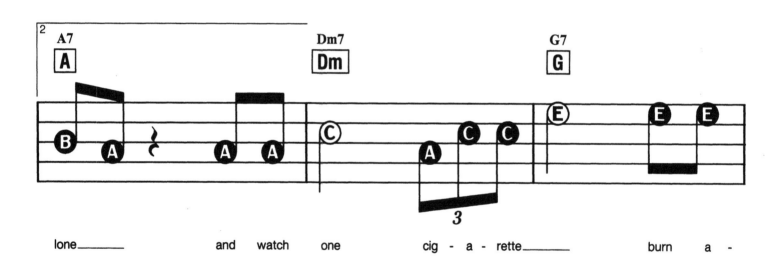

rette burn a - way.

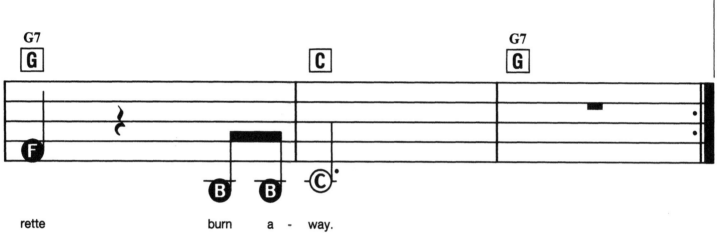

lone_____ and watch one cig - a - rette_____ burn a -

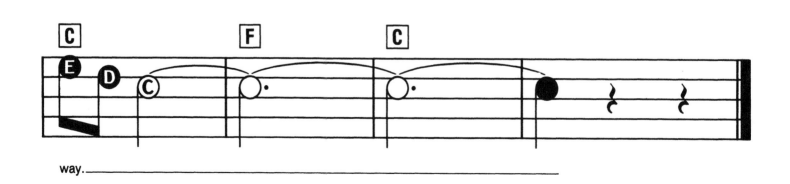

way._____

Walkin' After Midnight

Registration 1
Rhythm: Country, Pops, or Swing

Words and Music by
Don Hecht and Alan Block

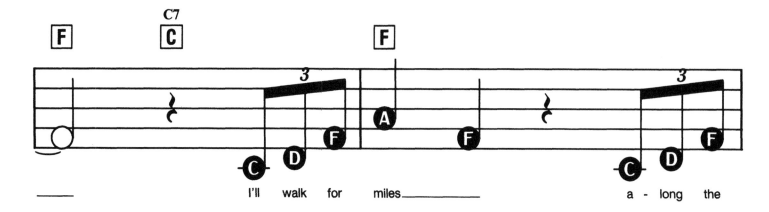

I'll walk for miles_____ a - long the

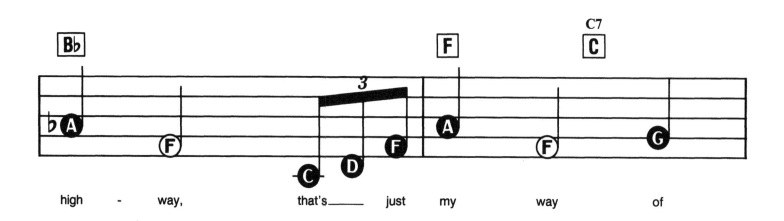

high - way, that's____ just my way of

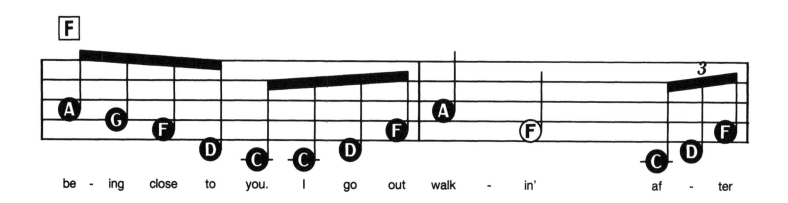

be - ing close to you. I go out walk - in' af - ter

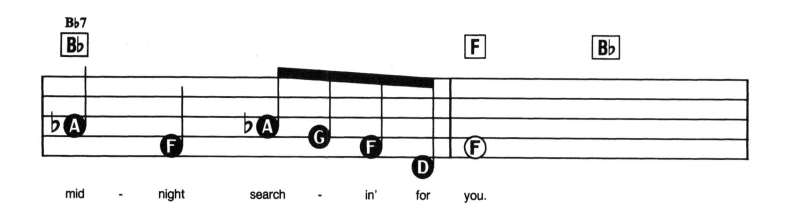

mid - night search - in' for you.

The Wayward Wind

Registration 4
Rhythm: Country or Shuffle

Words and Music by
Stan Lebowsky and Herbert Newman

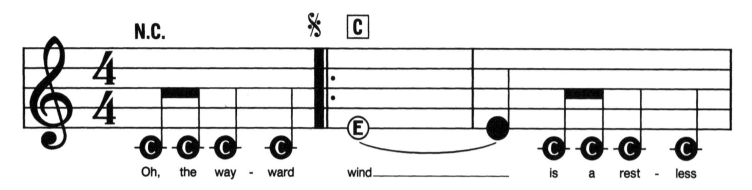

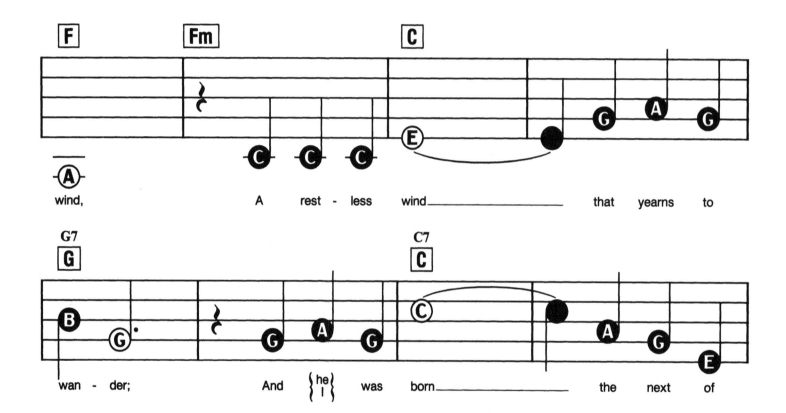

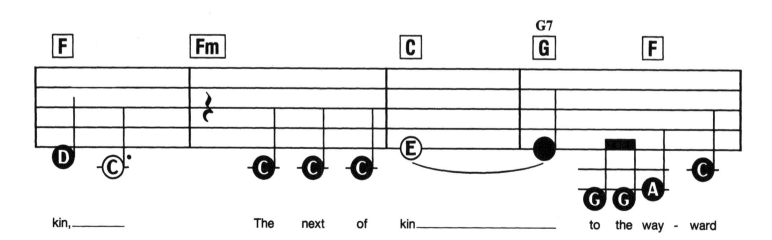

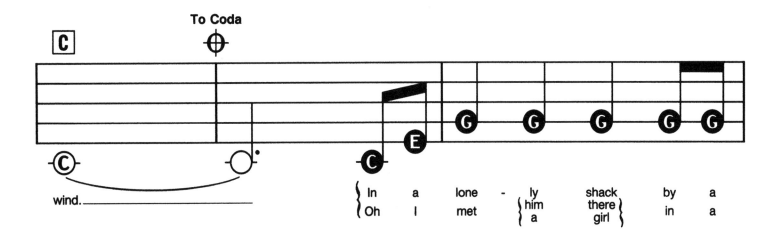

wind._____

In a lone - ly shack by a
Oh I met him a there in a

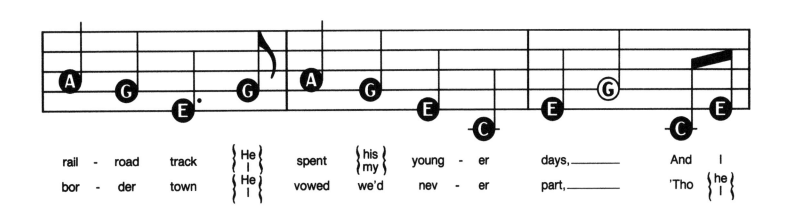

rail - road track He spent his young - er days, _____ And I
bor - der town He vowed we'd nev - er part, _____ 'Tho he

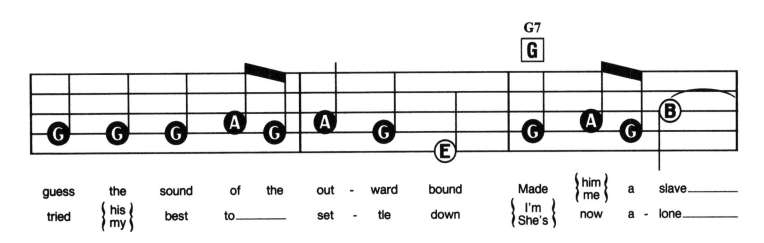

guess the sound of the out - ward bound Made him a slave _____
tried his best to _____ set - tle down I'm now a - lone _____

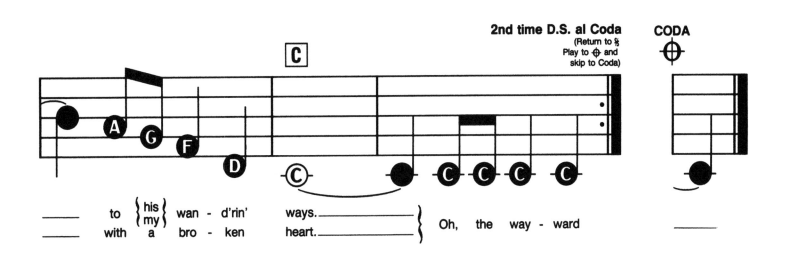

_____ to his wan - d'rin' ways. _____ Oh, the way - ward
_____ with a bro - ken heart. _____

When I Get Through With You
(You'll Love Me Too)

Registration 7
Rhythm: Swing, Pops, or Country

Words and Music by
Harland Howard

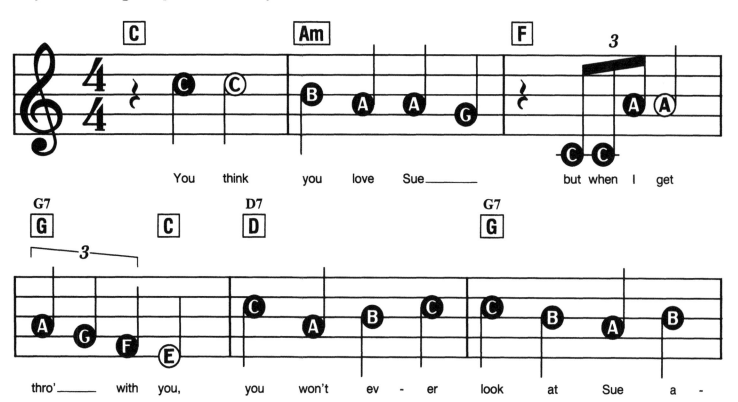

You think you love Sue_____ but when I get

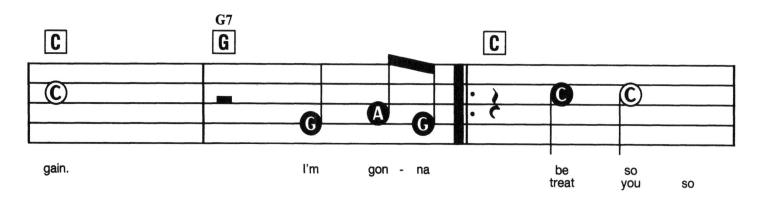

thro'_____ with you, you won't ev - er look at Sue a -

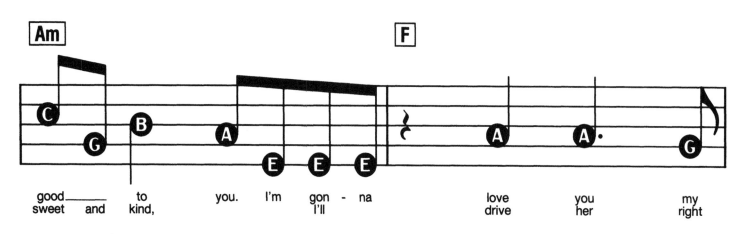

gain.   I'm gon - na   be so
                                    treat you so

good_____ to   you. I'm gon - na   love   you   my
sweet and   kind,   I'll   drive   her   right

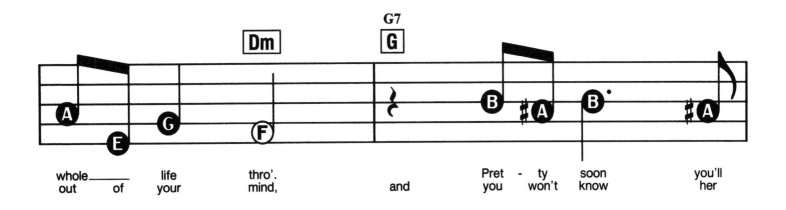

whole_____ life your thro'. mind, and Pret - ty soon you'll
out of your mind, you won't know her

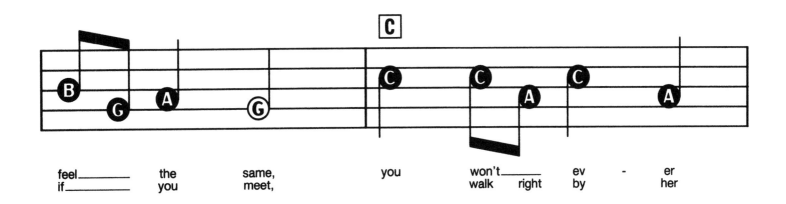

feel_____ the same, you won't_____ ev - er
if_____ you meet, walk right by her

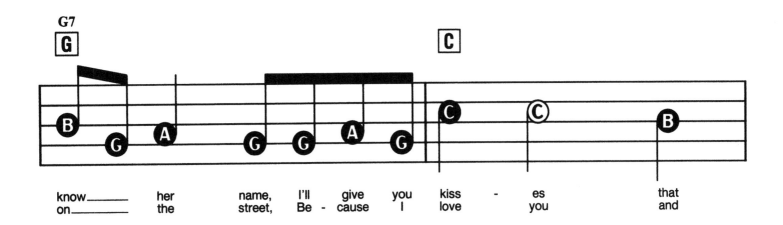

know_____ her name, I'll give you kiss - es that
on_____ the street, Be - cause I love you and

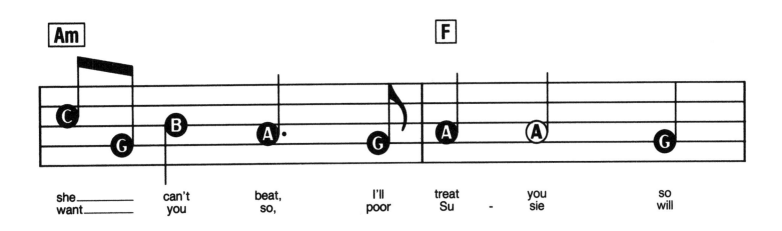

she_____ can't beat, so, I'll treat you so
want_____ you so, poor Su - sie will

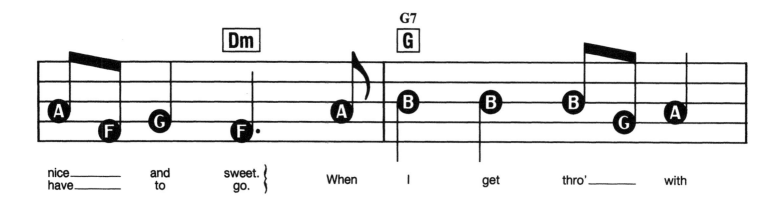

nice_____ and to sweet. }
have_____ to go. } When I get thro'_____ with

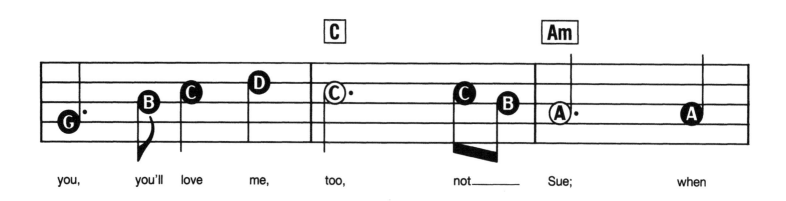

you, you'll love me, too, not_____ Sue; when

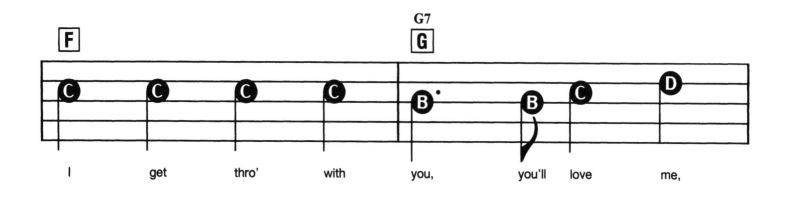

I get thro' with you, you'll love me,

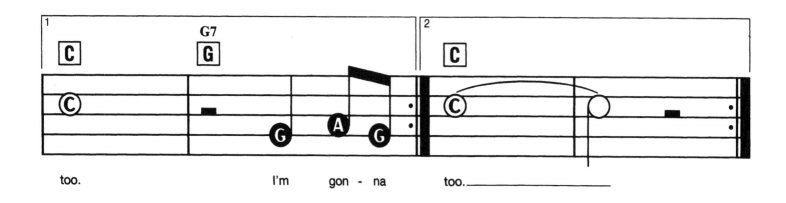

too. I'm gon - na too._____

Why Can't He Be You

Registration 9
Rhythm: Slow Rock or Swing

Words and Music by
Hank Cochran

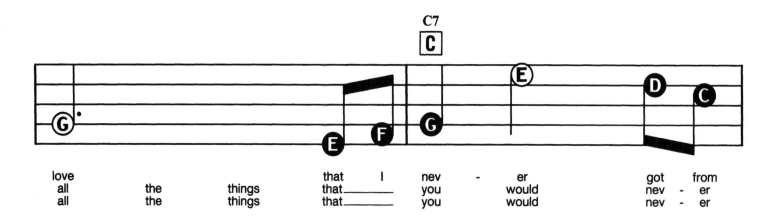

love | | | | that | I | nev | - | er | | got | from
all | | the | | things | that_____ | you | | would | | nev | - | er
all | | the | | things | that_____ | you | | would | | nev | - | er

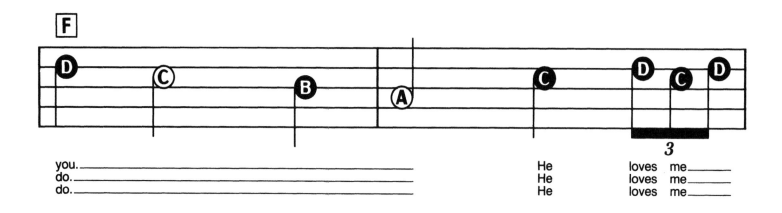

you._____ | | | | | | | He | loves | me_____
do._____ | | | | | | | He | loves | me_____
do._____ | | | | | | | He | loves | me_____

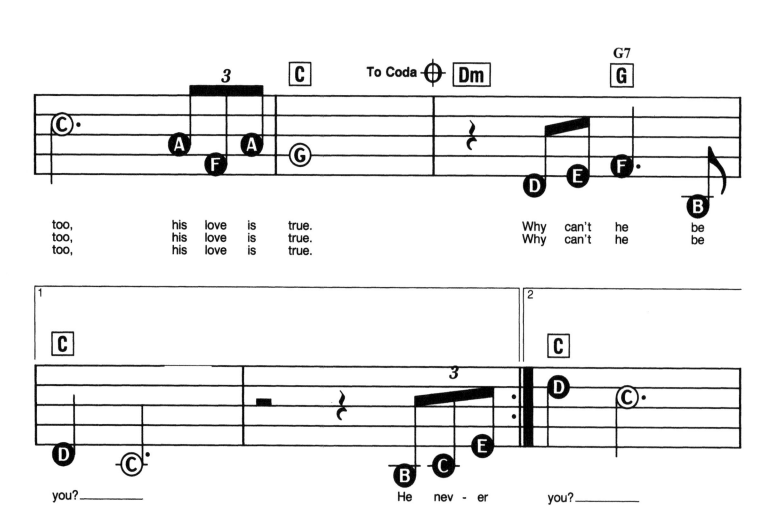

too, | | his | love | is | true. | | Why | can't | he | | be
too, | | his | love | is | true. | | Why | can't | he | | be
too, | | his | love | is | true.

you?_____ | | He | nev | - | er | | you?_____

Your Cheatin' Heart

Words and Music by
Hank Williams

Registration 5
Rhythm: Country or Ballad

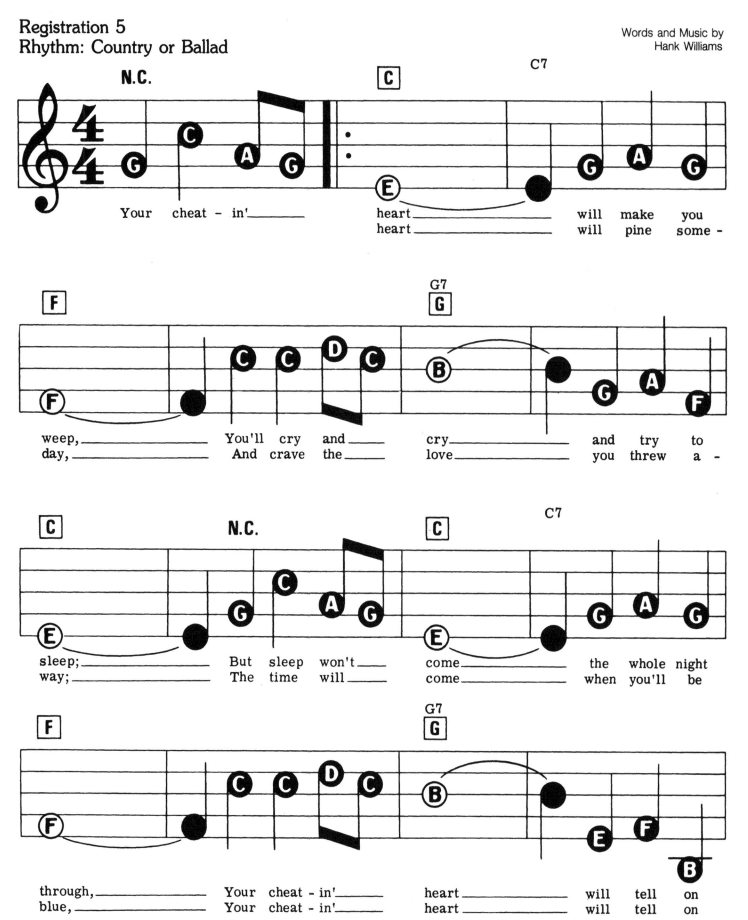

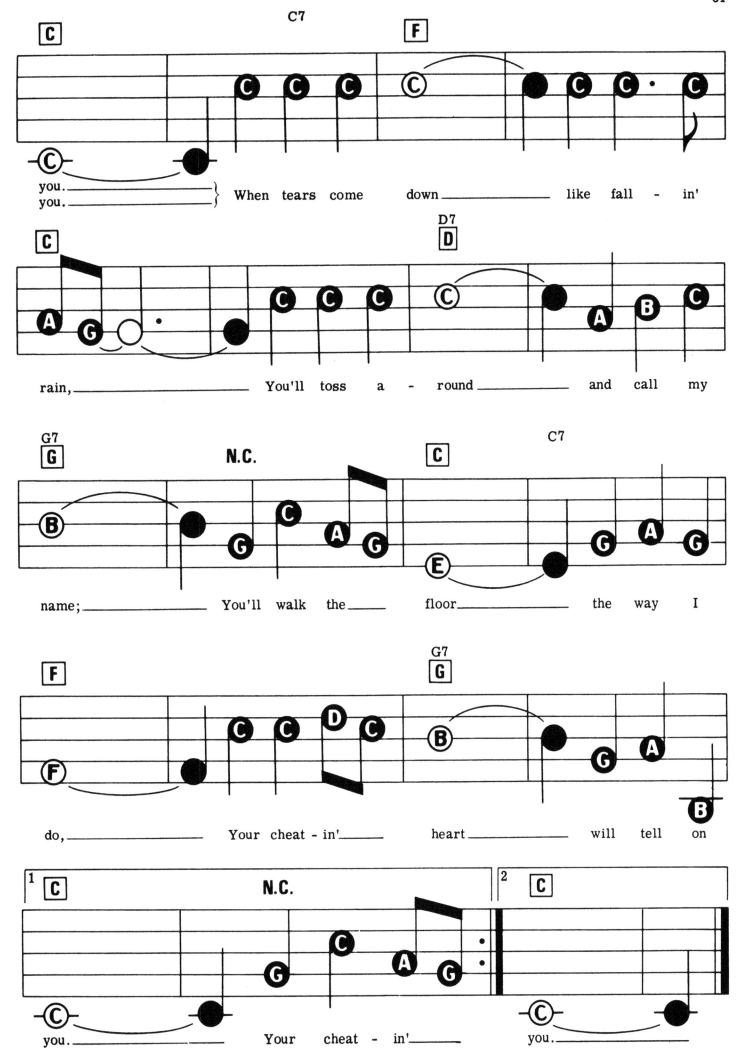

You're Stronger Than Me

Registration 5
Rhythm: Country or Fox-Trot

Words and Music by
Hank Cochran and Jimmy Key

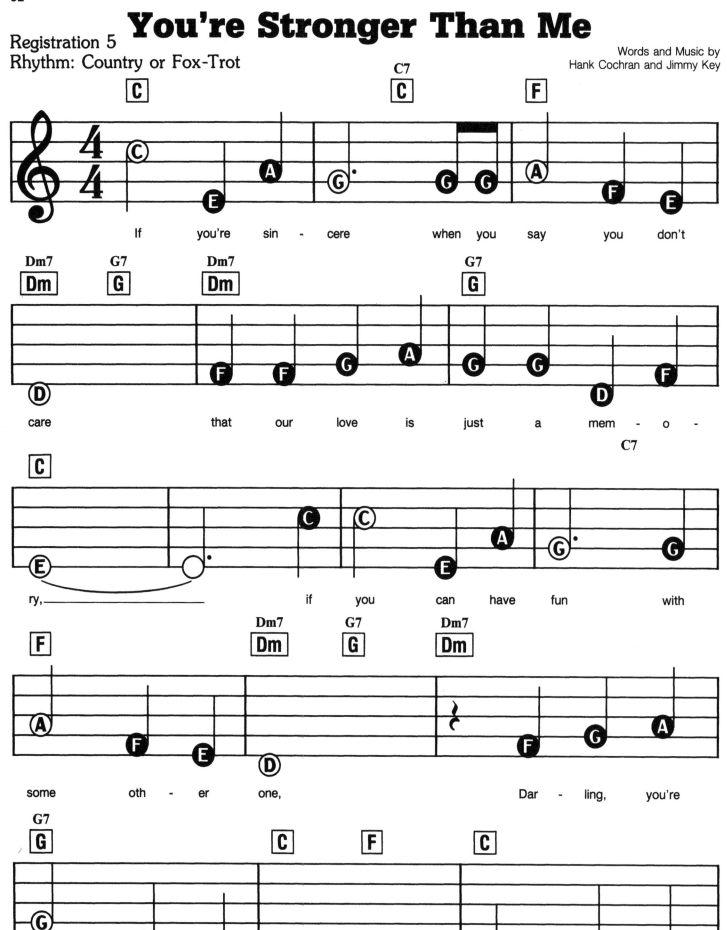

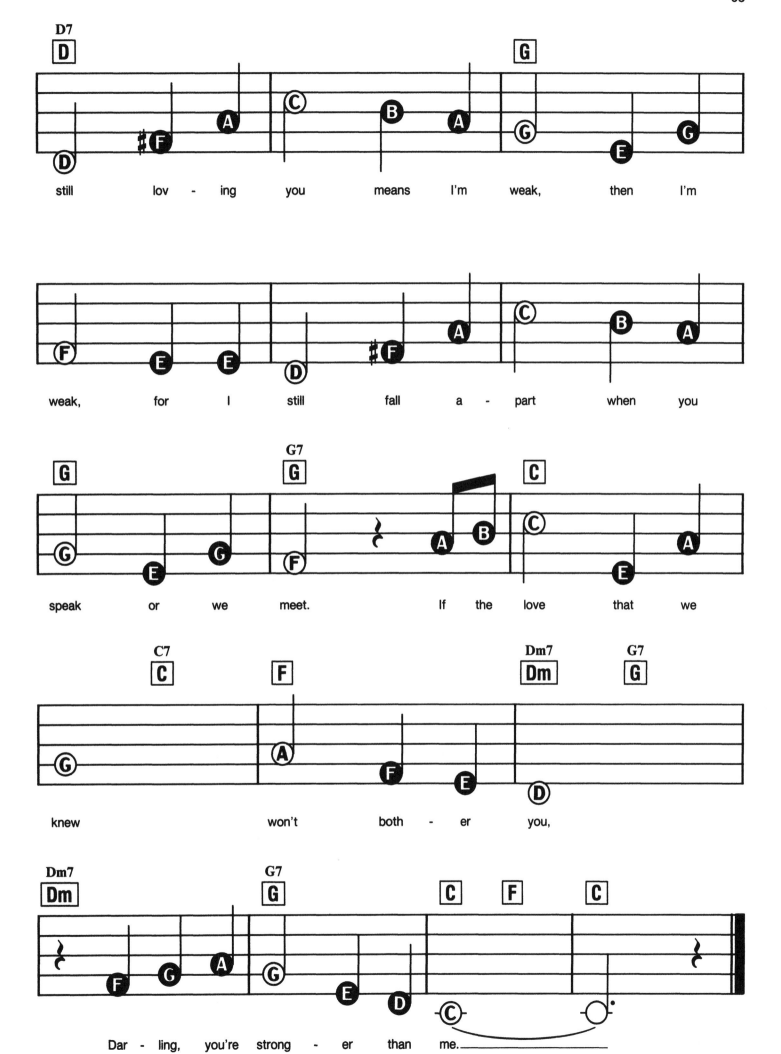

Registration Guide

- Match the Registration number on the song to the corresponding numbered category below. Select and activate an instrumental sound available on your instrument.

- Choose an automatic rhythm appropriate to the mood and style of the song. (Consult your Owner's Guide for proper operation of automatic rhythm features.)

- Adjust the tempo and volume controls to comfortable settings.

Registration

1	Flute, Pan Flute, Jazz Flute
2	Clarinet, Organ
3	Violin, Strings
4	Brass, Trumpet
5	Synth Ensemble, Accordion, Brass
6	Pipe Organ, Harpsichord
7	Jazz Organ, Vibraphone, Vibes, Electric Piano, Jazz Guitar
8	Piano, Electric Piano
9	Trumpet, Trombone, Clarinet, Saxophone, Oboe
10	Violin, Cello, Strings